Beauty for Free

Beauty for Free

A Compendium of Beauty Secrets
from Hearsay, History and Hedgerow

Catherine Palmer

JONATHAN CAPE
THIRTY BEDFORD SQUARE LONDON

First published 1981
Copyright © 1981 by Catherine Palmer
Jonathan Cape Ltd, 30 Bedford Square, London WC1

British Library Cataloguing in Publication Data

Palmer, Catherine
  Beauty for free
  1. Beauty, Personal
  I. Title
  646.7'2   RA778
  ISBN 0-224-01798-5

Printed in Great Britain by Butler & Tanner Ltd, Frome and London

Contents

Preface   9

INTRODUCTION   11
Drying and Storing Herbs and Flowers   15
Essential Oils   15
Stockists   16
General Hints   17
The Bain Marie   18
To make a Cream   18
To make an Infusion   18
A Decoction   19
To Distil   19
Prolonging the Life of Distilled Waters   19

THE FACE   21
Gathering the May Dew   23
Other Waters for the Complexion   23
   Scarlet Pimpernel water – Elderflower water – Daisy water – Plantain water – Lavender water – Periwinkle water Lettuce juice – Pomegranate juice – Turkish Poppy water – The Tears of the Vine – June water – Eyebright lotion – To remove freckles – Water of Cornflowers – Wild Strawberry water
Steaming the Face with Herbal Infusions   28
   Cleansing and soothing – A steam facial for oily skin – A stimulating steam facial for dull or sallow skin
Creams and Lotions   29
   Cowslips and cream – Chamomile cream – Cream of marigolds and lavender – Hollyhock cream – Galen's cold cream – Sandalwood lotion – Cream of witch-hazel, myrrh and bay – Yarrow cream – Princess of Wales – Old country recipes for elderflower ointment
Astringents   32
   Astringent for dry, sensitive skin – Astringent for oily skin – Flowery vinegar astringent – Pennyroyal vinegar – A Victorian water to preserve the colour of the skin
Face Masks   34
   Face mask to feed dry skin – Stimulating and tightening mask – Peppermint mask suitable for dry skin – Mask to remove dead skin and brighten the complexion – Deep cleansing mask for oily skin – Almond and honey mask for the bath
Benzoin   35
   Virgin milk – Schnouda, the rouge of the Arabian Nights
Make-Up   37
   Medieval face powder – Ancient Greek rouge – Chinese rouge – Lipstick – To darken the eyebrows – Rice powder

THE BODY   39
The Baths of Ancient Rome   41
   Rose unguent or Rhodium

More Luxurious Baths 42
The milk bath – The bath of modesty – Mme Tallier's bath – Ninon de l'Enclos's bath
Bath Oils 43
Huiles antiques – Bath oils using essential oils – Essential oils – Tropical bath oil – Mediterranean bath oil – Indian bath oil – Biblical bath oil
Herbs and Flowers in the Bath 46
Elecampane, mint and roses – High summer bath – The Wars of the Roses – Summer bath – A bath for aches and pains – Cottage garden bath – Herbal deodorants – Marie Antoinette's bath – Diane de Poitiers – The bath of Charles V of France

Massage Oils 48
A relaxing massage oil – An invigorating and refreshing massage oil
For Rough Skin and for the Neck 49
Paste of the Scythian Women – Rough skin lotion – Neck cream
The Sun 50
Sun oil for the tropics – Mediterranean sun oil
After-Sun Lotions to soothe Sunburn 51
Agar agar, witch-hazel and comfrey lotion – Elderflower water and glycerin – Anti-mosquito splash

Pregnancy 51
Anti-stretch mark oil – For the breasts – Lady's Mantle
Talcum Powder 53
Orange blossom and jasmine powder – Lavender and orris powder – Pink powder – New-mown hay powder
Almond Paste, or Hemsia 54
Almond paste
Soap 55
Rich moisturising soap – Honey and lemon soap – Soft herb soap – Napoleon's favourite soap – 'A delicate washing-ball' – 'To make an Ipswich ball' – 'A delicate wash-ball'

HAIR 59
Shampoo 61
Different Ways of making Shampoo 61
Shampoo for weak hair – Shampoo for all types of hair – Shampoo to stimulate growth – Peppermint shampoo for greasy hair – Shampoo for dry hair
Overhaul for Hair in Bad Condition 64
Neutral henna

Conditioning Rinses 65
  Rinse to add gloss, to encourage growth and to make the hair more manageable – Rinse for greasy hair – Rinse for dry hair
Tips for the Hair from Past and Present 65
  To curl the hair – To make it grow – An ointment to make the hair grow – To stop the hair from falling out – A medieval recipe to make the hair grow – Nettles to make the hair grow – Lemon juice – Rosemary and bay
Colour Rinses and Dyes 67
Red Hair and Golden Red Hair 67
  'To make the hair red' – 'To produce golden hair' – 'Capelli fila d'oro ...' – Saffron – Henna – To apply henna – Other dyes to mix with henna – Shampoo for red hair – Red rinse to follow – Marigold hair rinse – Virgin Mary gold – Strawberry blonde
Blonde Hair 70
  Chamomile dye – Chamomile, marigold and quassia rinse – 'To turn the Hair yellow' – 'To make the Hair fair and beautiful' – Blonde hair in Greece and Rome
Brown Hair Dyes 72
  Sage – Walnuts

HANDS AND FEET 73
Hands 75
  Finger nails – To colour the nails – Buffing the nails – The right and wrong days to cut nails – To make the half moons show on nails – To prevent redness of the hands – Wearing gloves at night – Dry oatmeal – To make the hands soft and white – Horse Chestnut paste for the hands – For cold and swollen hands – Mallow hand cream – Elderflower ointment for rough or chapped hands
Feet 77
  To help prevent your feet from looking old – Pumice stone – To prevent the cuticles from growing over the nails – Herbal foot baths – To prevent chilblains

SCENT 79
Ancient Egypt 81
  Kyphi – Other Egyptian perfumes
The Perfumes of Israel 84
  The Holy Anointing oil
Babylon, Nineveh and the Garden of Eden 84
  Eau de Ange
Greece 85
  To make a Huile antique – Maceration – A different scent for every part of the body
Rome 87
The Scents of the East 88
  Musk and roses – To make rose water – To make Attar of Roses – To preserve roses
Making Scent and Eau de Toilette using Essential Oils and Pure Alcohol 89
  Ethyl alcohol – Essential oils – Dark glass bottles – Glass droppers
Distillation 90
  Floral waters – To make concentrated flower waters – Another method
Enfleurage 91
The Middle Ages 91
  Eau de Chypre – Lavender water – Hungary water
The Perfumes of the Tudors 93
The Eighteenth Century 93
  Madame de Pompadour and Marie Antoinette – Eau de Cologne – Farina's Recipe

The Nineteenth Century   94
Rondeletia – Hovenia – Tea Rose – Water of Pinks – Other floral waters

POT POURRI AND SACHETS FOR CLOTHES   97
Pot pourri   99
Gathering flowers, drying and storing – To make pot pourri – Fixatives – Bay salt – A spicy carnation mixture – A very pretty mixture – Green pot porri – Rose pot pourri – New-mown hay – For the scent of orange groves – Eau de Cologne pot pourri – A pot pourri against the plague – Another germ killer
Sachets and other Dry Scents   104
To make sachets for clothes – Elizabeth I's 'Dry perfume' – 'Damask powder' – The 'Sachet powder' of Queen Isabella of Spain – 'A Violette powder for the perfuming of linen ...' – Indian shawls – 'White rose' sachet – 'Satan smells of sulphur and I smell of Orris root' – Flower sachets for the winter – Scented cupboards – Scented shells – To scent writing paper – Vetivert blinds – Scented cushions – 'A bag to smell unto for Melancholy ...' – A pillow filled with sleep-inducing herbs – A Citronella-scented candle to keep off insects and mosquitoes
Scenting the Room   108
Edward VI's Rose scent for the room – Juniper branches – Strewing the floor

MAGIC, CHARMS AND LOVE POTIONS   109
The Right Time to gather Magical Herbs   111
Magical Plants   112
The herbs of the Druids
Other Magical Plants of the Celts   113
Celtic Beauty   114
The Lay of the Nine Herbs   114
Charms, Fertility and Divinations of True Love   115
May Day   115
To conceive a child
Midsummer's Eve   116
To marry within the year ... – A cure for barrenness – To conjure up a midnight vision of your true love – To regain your lover's affections – To know if two people will love each other – 'A Midsummer Night's Dream'
Other Charms   118
A charm using Yarrow – To make your true love appear in a dream – To make your true love appear – A mirror and the moon
Love Potions   119
For making the true love powder – To ensure a happy marriage – Myrtle water – Mandrake and Bryony – Kissing comfits – Lettuce – Oranges and Orange blossom – Other plants used in love potions – 'Against the raging disease of love' – To cease weeping – Homer's Nepenthe

Appendix: Metric Conversion Tables   122
Picture Credits and Acknowledgments   123
A Select Bibliography   124
Index   125

Preface

As the study and use of herbs goes back into the mists of time, many ancient treatises have been written about them, and much folk-lore has been collected by scholars and researchers. Many writers have, over the years, added to the literature, so that any one working in this field today inevitably owes a debt to those who have gone before. At the end of my book I list the books which I have found particularly useful or interesting, but I would like to express my admiration of Hilda Leyel, author of *The Magic of Herbs*, and of Jeanne Rose, *The Herbal Body Book*; their work proved to be a sound cornerstone for my own research.

1981   C. P.

Illustrating Shakespeare's A Midsummer Night's Dream

Introduction

'Things are pretty, graceful, rich, elegant, handsome, but, until they speak to the imagination, not yet beautiful.' Emerson, 'Beauty', *The Conduct of Life*, 1860.

The glamour of herbs and rare spices, with their strange scents and magical associations, has nearly disappeared from modern life.

The aim of this book is to rediscover the old lore surrounding beauty, with its recipes and stories, and make that lost world easily accessible again.

The recipes come from ancient Egypt, Rome, and the harems of Arabia, from Renaissance Europe, English folk-lore and the present day. They all use natural ingredients which can be found in the hedgerows or the garden, or bought from herbalists and chemists, and have been updated to make them easy to follow. Botanical drawings of many of the plants are included.

Behind many of the recipes lies a tradition, once taken for granted, in which a feeling of harmony with nature, and a knowledge of her ways, went hand in hand with the quest for beauty. Others are included for their long-forgotten fame, and the legends that grew up around them: Eau de Chypre, brought back from the crusades in the time of Richard Cœur de Lion, Hungary Water, which gave Elizabeth of Hungary her ageless beauty, the rouge of the 'Arabian Nights', the first cold cream, scented with roses, invented by a Greek physician two thousand years ago.

Plants, for our ancestors, occupied an exalted place in the scheme of things. They were the only source of perfumes and cosmetics, as well as of healing. Attar of roses, frankincense, myrrh, cinnamon, have always been symbols of the precious and the hard to obtain, while even the commonest herb was infused with celestial energies and related to the stars. Although we no longer have our ancestors' knowledge, we can follow their recipes, gathering the ingredients in the right way, and at the right time, and mixing them, which puts us in touch again with the waxing and waning of the moon and the changing seasons.

The first perfumes and cosmetics we know of in the West were made by the Egyptians. They painted their eyes black with kohl, a powder made from antimony, and rouged their cheeks with finely powdered red ochre. After bathing they anointed themselves with scented oils made from origanum and bitter almonds, or from the exotic spices which they imported from Arabia. Their love of perfumes reached its height in the time of Cleopatra.

For the Greeks, perfumes had a divine origin. The appearance of a goddess on earth was always accompanied by a heavenly scent, which she shed around her – such a perfume alone was evidence of her presence – but, when Helen of Troy returned to Greece, she brought with her some of the secrets of Venus, to which she owed her fatal beauty, and the art of Greek perfumery began. Oil scented with roses was the first, but soon unguents and oils were prepared from wild mint, and from the irises of Elis, the roses of Paestum and Phaselis, the crocuses of Rhodes, and the apples and marjoram of Cos. The women of ancient Greece wore little make-up, using only the powdered root of alkanet to stain their cheeks and lips.

The Romans, on the other hand, painted their faces and dyed their hair with such violent dyes that many of them were reduced to wearing wigs of the fashionably blonde hair of their German captives.

The magical and astrological use of herbs and flowers, for both health and beauty, reached its height with the great occult herbalists of the Renaissance, and continued long after. According to astrology, which began in Babylon, each plant was governed by a planet, and possessed some of its powers; it had its place and its importance in a beautiful and ordered universe. For the Renaissance herbalists this universe was alive, and filled with invisible sympathies and antipathies. Heaven and earth reflected one another, and the inner properties of a plant were revealed by its outward form. The Doctrine of Signatures, as this belief was called, meant that for those with eyes to see the uses of each plant could be inferred from the shape of its leaves or the colour of its flowers.

The dividing line between magic and practical pharmacy was slim: plants were used as much for their hidden powers as for their cosmetic or medicinal value. The word cosmetic itself echoes their beliefs. It comes from the Greek, and means not only something which adorns, but also something which leads towards an ordered universe, a 'cosmos'.

These herbalists also paid attention to the mutual likes and dislikes of flowers. Poisons were seen to grow beside their antidotes, as the nettle

Sixteenth-century astronomers

grows beside the dock. Modern bio-dynamic gardening has found scientific evidence to support the findings of these old herbalists.

Alchemy also plays a part in the lore surrounding beauty; the distillation of scent was a part of the alchemists' search for the true gold, while the strange ingredients of their brews are found in many early recipes. Master Alexis the Piedmontese, in his medieval book of secrets, gives the following recipe, guaranteed to give eternal beauty: 'Take a young raven from its nest, feed it on hard eggs for forty days, kill it, and distil it with myrtle leaves, talc, and almond oil.' Both ravens and eggs were common symbols of alchemical death and rebirth.

From the wealth of recipes for scent and cosmetics to be found in old books and manuscripts, I have chosen those which are easy to do, and which convey most vividly a sense of mystery, or of participation with nature. They are also practical, and work well.

The modern recipes I have included are also easy to do. They contain natural herbs and oils which are more beneficial to the skin than many modern cosmetics, and far cheaper. They, like the older recipes, belong to a tradition, in which much is being discovered all the time.

Drying and Storing Herbs and Flowers

All plants should be harvested on a fine day in summer after the morning dew has gone, but before the sun is hot. If you leave it until the afternoon much of the scent will have gone. Use a knife, or break off the leaves and flowers carefully, so that they do not get too bruised, and dry them in a warm, dry place in the shade; an airing cupboard is ideal. You can stretch some net over a wooden frame and spread the plants thinly over it, or you can put them on newspaper if there is plenty of ventilation under the plants.* Once they have become crisp and dry, but not powdery, put them in well-sealed dark glass jars, or sealed paper bags, and store in the cool, away from direct light.

Alternatively, whole plants can be tied together at the base with string, and hung upside down in a dark warm place to dry; the juices of the plant drain down into the leaves, and so you get the maximum benefit from them.

Essential Oils

The essential oils of plants, which contain the scent of the plant in its most concentrated form, are extracted by various methods: distillation and enfleurage, both of which can be done on a small scale at home (see pages 90, 91), being two of them. They can be added to oil to make a scented bath oil, or to Ethyl alcohol to make scent or eau de toilette.

Many of the products sold under the name of essential oils are synthetic. On the whole the oils made from herbs tend to be genuine, as the whole plant can be used, while those made from the flowers alone tend to be synthetic; pure rose, jasmine and tuberose fetch thousands of pounds a kilo, and are not sold retail. However, many of the synthetic oils do not differ chemically in any way from the oils they imitate, and they are, of course, far cheaper.

---

*They should be turned every day or so to make sure that they dry evenly, and never be piled on top of each other.

Stockists

G. BALDWIN & CO., 173, Walworth Road, Elephant & Castle, London SE17, stock the following ingredients mentioned in this book, and many others:

agar agar
alkanet root
avocado oil
bay salt
beeswax, white and yellow
calamus root
cocoa butter
galingale root

gum arabic
Irish moss
myrrh and frankincense, to order
quince seeds
orris root
tonquin beans
turkey red oil

ESSENTIAL OILS
bergamot
cassia
cedarwood
citronella
chamomile
frangipani
frankincense
gardenia
jasmine
lavender

lemon balm
lemongrass
lily
mimosa
orange flower
rose
rosemary
thyme
tuberose

They do not do mail order.

CULPEPER LTD, 21, Bruton Street, London W1, have an enormous range of herbs, and also stock:

allspice berries
apricot kernel oil
essential oil of peppermint

liquorice sticks
peach kernel oil

MOST HEALTH FOOD SHOPS will stock:

agar agar
ginseng root and elixir

henna
hibiscus flowers
liquorice sticks

Common Chamomile

sesame oil
sunflower oil

vitamin E capsules
wheatgerm oil

BOOTS stock:

coconut oil
kaolin
'Simple Soap'

talcum powder (unscented)

BOOTS AND MOST CHEMISTS stock:

almond oil
alum

borax
clove oil

16

fuller's earth
glycerin
kaolin powder
lanolin
orange flower water
rose water

'Simple Soap'
talcum powder
  (unscented)
Vaseline
vitamin E capsules
witch-hazel

THE AROMATIC OIL CO., 12 Littlegate Street, Oxford (mail order), stock the following essential oils, and many others:

bay
benzoin
bergamot
cedarwood
chamomile
cypress
frankincense
geranium
hyssop

jasmine
lavender
lemon
myrrh
orange
rose
rosemary
sage
sandalwood

THE COTSWOLD PERFUMERY, Bourton-on-the-Water, Glos., will supply Ethyl alcohol with half a per cent of perfume added, by mail order. They will also supply glass droppers for perfumery.

COUNTRY COTTAGE NATURAL COSMETICS, The Banks, Birches Lane, Newent, Glos., will provide the following by mail order:
harmless chemical preservatives suitable for all cosmetics and distilled waters.

alkanet root
avocado oil
beeswax
calamus root
cocoa butter

galingale root
Irish moss
quince seeds
tonquin beans
turkey red oil

They will also supply entire kits for making creams and lotions, containing all the necessary ingredients, including chemical preservatives. Apply to the above address for more details.

General Hints

When making your own cosmetics, or infusing and distilling herbs, always use enamel saucepans, china bowls and wooden spoons. Metal utensils will spoil them.

Unless you are using a chemical preservative, or making a scent which contains at least 20 per cent alcohol, it is essential to follow the following rules when making creams, lotions, or distilled waters:

1 Conditions should be as sterile as possible; jars or bottles should be sterilised by immersing them in warm water, bringing them to the boil and simmering for three minutes before using them to store creams and distilled waters.
2 Containers should be made either out of dark

glass or opaque plastic, as strong light will make them go off quicker.

3 The finished product should be stored in a cool dark place, and not exposed to violent changes of temperature. Once opened, if they are kept in the fridge it will prolong their life, but this is by no means necessary for many things.

4 Never make more of anything perishable than you can use up quickly.

5 Always have clean hands before using creams or distilled waters, as the germs you introduce will make them go bad more quickly.

Vitamin E, or wheatgerm oil have been added to all the creams and lotions both for their beneficial effects on the skin, and to help preserve them.*

In the past, people did not expect many of their cosmetics to last a long time, and they tended to use whatever was in season if there was any question of its going bad. Having said this, however, there are many things which will last well, and the others can be made as you need them, so don't be discouraged.

The Bain Marie – for making Creams and Lotions, Soaps and Shampoos

You will need a large saucepan, a china bowl which fits into the top of it to form a Bain Marie and another china bowl, slightly larger than the first.

To make a Cream

Place the oil, the beeswax, and the lanolin or cocoa butter, if used, in the smaller china basin, and suspend it over the saucepan, which should be half filled with boiling water. Put the saucepan on the heat, and wait for all the ingredients to melt. Stir to mix if necessary. When they have melted, remove the china basin from the saucepan, and add the liquid (the rose water, or herbal infusion) drop by drop, beating all the while with a wooden spoon, as you would for mayonnaise. When all the liquid has been added, drop in the essential oil to scent the mixture and the vitamin E. (Choose the larger variety of vitamin E capsule which can be pricked with a pin, and the contents easily squeezed out.) Suspend the bowl over the larger bowl, which should be half full of cold water. Continue beating, and the cream will begin to solidify, and lose its oily appearance. It is very easy to tell when the cream is finished. Spoon into a dark glass or opaque plastic jar, and put on the lid.

Creams and lotions vary slightly in their ingredients, but they consist basically of an oil, and a liquid (such as rose water). Many of them also contain a greasy substance such as lanolin, which adds body to the cream and nourishes the skin, while beeswax is added to make the mixture firmer. Vitamin E is added both for its beneficial effects on the skin, and to help preserve the cream or lotion. Essential oils are added for scent, and for the properties of the plant from which they are extracted.

To make an Infusion

Pour a cupful of boiling water over half an ounce of dried herbs, or a handful of fresh ones (dried

---

* If you use a chemical preservative in your creams and lotions the vitamin E can be omitted or reduced to make a lighter cream.

herbs are more concentrated); using a non-metallic saucepan, simmer the herbs with the lid on for one minute, then remove from the heat and allow to stand, covered, for up to twenty minutes, depending on how strong you wish the infusion to be. If you want a really strong one, leave the herbs to infuse until the liquid is cool. Strain and keep in the refrigerator.

A Decoction

The word decoction is used to describe an infusion made with roots, dried berries, or bark. As they are harder than flowers, it takes more to get the goodness out of them, so place them in an enamel saucepan, cover well with water, and simmer gently for twenty minutes to half an hour with the lid on. Strain, and keep in the refrigerator.

To Distil

You will need a large enamel saucepan that has a rounded lid, and does not have a plastic handle (plastic will spoil the scent), a smaller bowl, preferably Pyrex, or something that can take heat, a round rack to stand the bowl on, not made of metal, some small, smooth stones and some ice.

Place the rack in the centre of the saucepan and stand the bowl on it. Put the stones around the rack so that they evenly cover the bottom of the saucepan; they will stop the flowers from burning. Lay the flowers or leaves over the stones, and cover with water. You want enough water to prevent the flowers from burning, but not so much as to make the scent weak.

Put the saucepan on the heat, and place the lid on upside down. When the water begins to boil,

fill the up-turned lid with ice. As the steam rises it will meet the cold lid, condense, run down towards the centre of the lid, and fall into the bowl. What comes into the bowl is a distilled water of flowers. Different plants vary in the speed at which the scent will come over into the bowl, so the best thing is to experiment: After five minutes remove the bowl, being careful not to let any steam escape from the saucepan, pour the contents into a cup over which boiling water has previously been poured to help sterilise it, and put it in the fridge, covered, until it is cool. Replace the bowl in the saucepan and repeat the process. If the second batch is as strongly scented as the first it is worth repeating the process a third time, if not, be content with what you have got. Pour into a dark glass bottle, and put the lid on immediately.

Prolonging the Life of Distilled Waters

There are various ways of prolonging the life of these distilled waters:

1 Ethyl Alcohol and Glycerin

Add 20 per cent of Ethyl alcohol and 15 per cent of glycerin to a distilled water that is to be used on the face. The alcohol will preserve the water, and the glycerin will counteract much of the astringent effect of alcohol on the skin, without making the mixture sticky. Many aftershaves for men and astringents for women contain up to 20 per cent alcohol, but they are best suited to oily skin, as they can cause irritation when used on dry or sensitive skin despite the presence of the glycerin. If you do have dry or sensitive skin, use one of the methods below. Alcohol is also unsuitable as a preservative for waters distilled from emollient or soothing herbs, as it acts as a powerful astringent, and so cancels out the properties of the herb. If you wish to use the flower water as an eau de toilette and not as a face lotion, the glycerin should be omitted, as the alcohol will do no harm on other parts of the body.

2 Chemical Preservatives

Some harmless preservatives, similar to those used in food, are available (see list of stockists), which can be used in minute quantities to preserve your floral waters, creams and lotions.

3 The Fridge

This method is not so efficient as the other two, but it does have the advantage of giving you a completely pure product. The bottle, which must be made of dark glass or some opaque material, must be sterilised by immersion in warm water which is then brought to the boil and simmered for 3 minutes. When you have finished distilling, pour the liquid into this bottle, making sure that the liquid comes very near the top, as the presence of air makes the liquid go off, and put the lid on immediately. When the essential oil has separated from the water, and floated to the top, remove it with a cotton bud, and replace the lid. If the liquid reaches the top of the bottle, this should keep for several weeks unopened. Once opened, make sure that your hands are clean before using it, as bacteria which make the water go bad are introduced very easily. As you use it, you can drop clean marbles into the bottle to keep the liquid level with the top of the bottle. Stored in the fridge this should last another few weeks. If you are going to follow this method it is best to make only a small amount at a time.

The Face

'There is a garden in her face,
Where roses and white lilies grow ... '
Thomas Campion

Gathering the May Dew

Since time out of mind girls have gone out before dawn on May Day and gathered the May Dew to wash their faces in. It was believed to give a beautiful complexion, and to remove freckles and other blemishes, as well as to bring luck for the year ahead. Here is the proper way of doing it from *Ram's Little Dodoen*, printed in 1606:

> When there hath fallen no raine the night before, then with a cleane and large sponge, the next morning, you may gather the same from sweet herbs, grasse or corne: straine your dew, and expose it to the Sun in glasses covered with papers or parchments prickt full of holes; straine it often, continuing it in the Sun, and in a hot place, till the same grow white and cleare, which will require the best part of the Summer.
>
> Some commend May-Dew, gathered from Fennell and Celandine to be most excellent for sore eyes ...

Other methods do not take all summer; you can gather the dew with a clean muslin cloth, and then squeeze it into a china bowl for use.

Other Waters for the Complexion

One of the simplest and cheapest ways of having a good complexion is to wash your face with water made from flowers and herbs. It is easier to make an infusion (see page 18), but if you want to keep it for longer than a few days, distil it in the home-made still described on page 19.

Gathering the mountain dew on May Day morning

Scarlet Pimpernel. Common on cultivated land, waste land, and on the dunes. Flowers May–August

Scarlet Pimpernel Water

One of the great standbys of the past, it was to be found on every woman's dressing table. It is cleansing, slightly astringent, clears spots and freckles, and was considered a 'sovereign remedy' for whitening the complexion.

Gather a handful of the small star-shaped red flowers, without the stalks, and either infuse or distil.

Scarlet Pimpernel's Latin name, *Anagallis*, means delightful, probably because of its reputation for dispelling melancholy. To hold a sprig in your hand is supposed to give second sight, and the power to understand the speech of birds and animals. You will certainly be able to predict the weather while you are picking these flowers. They are also called the Shepherd's Glass, because they open only on sunny days, and close soon after the sun disappears.

Elderflower Water

This is the most famous of all the cosmetic waters. It is both healing and gently astringent, and so is suitable for normal or dry skin. Culpeper says that this plant of Venus clears sunburn and freckles, and will soothe bloodshot eyes if they are washed with it. It is good for the pores and whitens the skin.

Gather the flowers when they are just coming to their prime, discard the stalks, and either infuse or distil.

The scent of the water is nicer than that of the fresh flowers, as anyone who has drunk elderflower champagne will know, and they grow plentifully, so you will have no trouble finding some.

The elder tree has always been treated with great respect in northern countries. It was a tree of power; before cutting its wood, which was never burned, men would ask permission of its indwelling spirit, the Lady of the Elder. It could be either good or evil, depending on how you behaved towards it.

Its Latin name, *Sambucus nigra*, is supposed to come from a musical instrument made from its wood.

Daisy Water

Water made from the daisy, or the day's eye as it is still called in south-western Scotland, is another cure for a bad complexion. Also ruled by Venus, it was used for skin diseases, to remove blotches, and to whiten the skin. The daisy was Chaucer's favourite flower:

> ... of al the floures in the mede,
> Thanne love I most thise floures white and rede,
> Swiche as men callen daysyes in our toun.

Plantain Water

The Red Indians called this plant of Venus 'Englishman's Foot', as it seemed to spring up in his footsteps when he arrived in the New World.

The whole plant can be used as a healing wash for bruised or inflamed skin. Its healing properties were inferred, according to the Doctrine of Signatures (which sees in the appearance and behaviour of a plant its probable uses for man) from its power to spring up again however badly it is crushed or bruised.

Lavender Water

Gather the flowers just before they are fully out, and when the dew is off them. Either distil or make an infusion of them.

The Romans used the lavender from their northern dominions to scent their bath water and their linen.

A plant of Mercury, the god, or planet, who

Greater Plantain. Common on lawns and in fields

rules all kinds of travel and 'mercurial' thoughts, lavender water is said to soothe nervous headaches, and to calm and clear the mind.

For the skin, it is disinfectant and refreshing and it has a beautiful scent.

Periwinkle Water, or Water of Sorcerer's Violets

Use the fresh leaves to make an infusion or a distillation. It is soothing, healing, and astringent, and was often used in love philtres, being a plant of fertility. In medieval Italy and England wreaths of periwinkles were hung around the necks of those about to be executed, possibly as a promise of rebirth. Both the greater and the lesser periwinkles, *Vinca major* and *Vinca minor*, can be used as a wash.

Lettuce Juice

The lettuce is sacred to Adonis, god of the returning spring, and is ruled by the Moon, as are all cool and watery things; the cucumber is another, and it soothes sunburn. It is also good for pimply skin, or for any roughness or soreness. Scald the lettuce with a little boiling water, and squeeze out the juice.

Culpeper says that the juice, mixed with oil of roses (see page 86), 'applied to the forehead and temples, procures sleep'. The gypsies still eat fresh lettuce leaves for the same reason, and the Anglo-Saxons called it Sleep-wort.

Pomegranate Juice

Squeeze the juice from a pomegranate, and use it as a mild astringent lotion if you have an oily skin.

The pomegranate is one of the oldest symbols of

Red Poppy. The wild poppy, also called the Corn Rose, is still common in cornfields and along the wayside. Flowers May–July

fertility; the Empress of the Tarot cards holds one in her hand, along with a sheaf of corn; but it is most famous as the fruit of Proserpine, goddess of the underworld. It was because she ate the pomegranate offered her by Hades, which Keats called 'the ruby grapes of Proserpine', that she was forced to return to the underworld for part of the year, and winter was created.

Turkish Poppy Water

In Turkey today, women make a water of red poppies in the following way: place several handfuls of red poppy petals in a china bowl, squeeze over them the juice of a lemon, sprinkle them with sugar, and cover them with rain water, or pure spring water. The bowl is then placed, covered with a muslin cloth, on the roof of the house overnight, in the cool air, and brought indoors before the heat of the day begins. It is then strained and used as a general panacea for the complexion. If you don't have a flat roof use the window-ledge. The water should be used immediately, any remainder being kept in the fridge.

The Tears of the Vine

The sap of the vine, which in Latin is called *lachrymae*, or tears, was once used as an eye lotion for weak eyes. It can also be used on the face. An old source tells us to 'catch the drops which distil from the vine in the month of May and June, and wash your face with them'.

June Water

In Gloucestershire rain water, or June Water, as it is called, is still used to brighten the eyes. The rain must fall straight from heaven into a china bowl placed out of doors, the water then being used to wash the eyes.

Eyebright Lotion

Make an infusion or distillation of Eyebright (*Euphrasia officinalis* or *nemerosa*), and wash your eyes with it to brighten them and strengthen the sight.

Eyebright is ruled, suitably enough, by the light-giving sun.

To Remove Freckles

'Wash the face in the wane of the moon with a sponge, morning and evening, with the distilled water of elder leaves, letting the same dry into the skin. Your water must be distilled in May. This from a traveller who hath cured himself thereby.' Sir Hugh Platt, *Delights for Ladies*, 1609.

Water of Cornflowers

Make a distilled water or an infusion from the petals of cornflowers, which were once as common in cornfields as poppies; and use it as a refreshing water to wash your face with. It is still sold in France for this purpose.

Wild Strawberry Water

This is an old cosmetic water for removing spots and freckles. The fruit alone can be distilled, which smells delicious, or the whole plant.

There are many other herbs and flowers which are good for the complexion, and many ways of using them. One of the best is a steam facial.

Steaming the Face with Herbal Infusions

Cleansing and Soothing ...

Make a strong infusion of herbs, by placing a couple of handfuls of fresh leaves or flowers, or a couple of tablespoons of dried ones, in a china basin, and covering them with boiling water. Cover your head, and the basin, with a large towel, and allow the steam to act on your skin for about ten minutes, keeping your eyes closed. Try the following mixtures:

This mixture is cleansing and soothing for dry and sensitive skins ... it is also calming to the mind, and so an all-round relaxer.

1 teaspoon powdered liquorice root (to open the pores)
1 teaspoon (dried) comfrey leaves
1 teaspoon (powdered) comfrey root
2 teaspoons (dried) yellow chamomile
2 teaspoons (dried) lavender flowers
2 teaspoons (dried) lime blossoms (linden)

Splash your face with cold water after steaming, to close the pores.

You won't find all these things in flower at the same time, but use what fresh ones you can find, putting in larger amounts of these, and smaller amounts of the dried ones.

Comfrey, a herb of Saturn, is both astringent and emollient. It is one of the great healers, said to promote the growth of skin cells, regenerating ageing skin and healing wounds. The word comfrey is thought to come indirectly from the Latin 'confervere', to grow together.

Chamomile, with its warm and gentle scent, was dedicated to the sun by the Egyptians. It is one of the most gentle and healing of the herbs, reducing puffiness of the skin, and also strengthening and cleansing it.

Lavender (see Lavender water above), is antiseptic, tonic and calming, both mentally and physically.

Lime blossoms are cooling to the skin, and antiseptic, while they also help counteract hysteria and general overactivity of the nervous system.

This mixture is also good for pimples and spots.

A Steam Facial for Oily Skin

Make a strong infusion of the following herbs, and follow the instructions given above:

1 tablespoon fresh blackberry leaves
1 tablespoon fresh costmary
1 handful of rose petals
1 tablespoon fresh leaves of lady's mantle

Blackberry leaves are used to soothe burns. They are astringent.

Costmary, an old herb with a very pleasant scent, was used to flavour ale and to preserve linen. It is good for oily skin, and is antiseptic.

Lady's mantle is tightening, healing and astringent.

Splash your face with cold water after steaming, to close the pores.

A Stimulating Steam Facial for Dull or Sallow Skin

Make a strong infusion of the following herbs, and follow the instructions above:

2 tablespoons of scented rose geranium leaves (fresh)
4 tablespoons mint leaves (fresh)
1 tablespoon marigold petals (fresh)

Spike Lavender. Flowers July and August

Splash your face with cold water and lemon juice afterwards, to close the pores.

Mint and rose geranium are both stimulating and astringent to the skin, and deliciously scented.

Marigolds are stimulating and healing. Lemon juice helps to remove old skin cells, which cause sallow skin.

Creams and Lotions

Cowslips and Cream

It has been said that 'really fresh cream' is the best moisturiser of all, but you can add to it by stirring in two tablespoons of a strong infusion of cowslip flowers, whose reputation for clearing the skin, and brightening it, dates from very early days.

Chamomile Cream

For puffy skin, and to strengthen the tissues.

- 1 tablespoon coconut oil
- 3 tablespoons almond oil
- 2 tablespoons strong chamomile infusion
- 1 teaspoon white beeswax
- 5 drops essential oil of chamomile
- 5 capsules vitamin E (contents of: use the larger variety which have a soft covering that can easily be pricked with a pin)

To make, follow the instructions given on page 18 (Bain Marie).

This is a pale, golden cream, and its scent is reminiscent of the chamomile lawns and seats of old-fashioned summer gardens.

Cream of Marigolds and Lavender

- 1 tablespoon lanolin
- 3 tablespoons almond oil
- 2 tablespoons strong marigold infusion
- 1 teaspoon white beeswax

5 capsules vitamin E (contents of)
5 drops essential oil of lavender

Marigolds are one of the most healing herbs for the skin.

Follow the instructions given on page 18 (Bain Marie).

Hollyhock Cream

Hollyhocks, like mallows to which they are related, are softening and emollient.

1 tablespoon cocoa butter (oil of theobroma)
3 tablespoons almond oil
2 tablespoons hollyhock infusion
5 capsules vitamin E (contents of)

Follow the instructions for the creams above.

Galen's Cold Cream

The first cold cream was invented by a Greek physician, Galen, two thousand years ago: Galen melted four ounces of white wax in a pound of rose oil. When the mixture was melted, it was poured from one vessel to another, and a small amount of water was gradually stirred in, which gave the cream its whiteness. A little rose water and rose vinegar were then added.

Ancient Greek oil of roses is made in the following way: macerate twelve ounces of highly scented rose buds in four ounce relays in olive oil over a period of days, and then strain.

You can make the real *huile antique* of roses, as Galen did, and follow his recipe, but halve or even quarter the amount, unless you want a big supply!

Here is a more modern version of the same cream, made in the way described on page 18 (Bain Marie).

3 tablespoons olive oil
2 teaspoons white beeswax
1 tablespoon rose water
5 drops essential oil of roses

Sandalwood Lotion

To rejuvenate the skin.

1 tablespoon lanolin
3 dessertspoons wheatgerm oil

3 dessertspoons almond oil
2 tablespoons strong comfrey leaf infusion
2 vitamin E capsules (contents of)
5 drops essential oil of sandalwood

Follow the instructions given on page 18 (Bain Marie).

Made from all the things that rejuvenate the skin, and feed it, this cream is scented with sandalwood, which Septimus Piesse, the famous perfumer, believed to be one of the seven primary odours. Apart from its use as a scent, which dates back to the fifth century B.C. in India, where the wood was also used to build temples, it is wonderful for both dry and oily skin. It relieves irritation, and is thought to rejuvenate the skin. Sandalwood was the general panacea of ancient India.

Cream of Witch-hazel, Myrrh and Bay

For oily skin.

1 tablespoon cocoa butter
3 tablespoons almond oil
2 tablespoons witch-hazel
2 or 3 drops each of essential oils of myrrh and bay

Follow the instructions given on page 18 (Bain Marie).

This is a strangely scented creamy lotion. Witch-hazel, or hamamelis water, is both cleansing and astringent, and also good for bruised or inflamed skin. Bay, the tree of Apollo, is stimulating and healing for bruised skin, while myrrh, so popular in ancient Egypt for its preservative qualities, and extolled in the Song of Solomon for its scent, is a local antiseptic, healing and astringent.

Daphne and Apollo

The infant Achilles bathed in the Styx

Yarrow Cream

Yarrow is called *Achillea millefolium* after Achilles, who is supposed to have tended his soldiers' wounds with it. It was used by the Anglo-Saxons to heal wounds inflicted by iron. It is cleansing and astringent. The women of the Scottish highlands also used it as a charm to ensure a 'glad voice', 'warm lips' and a 'sweet figure'. In Berwick it is known as 'melancholy', and in Wiltshire as 'Traveller's Ease'. It is a plant of divination.

1 teaspoon white beeswax
3 tablespoons almond oil
2 tablespoons strong yarrow infusion
5 vitamin E capsules (contents of)

Follow the instructions given on page 18 (Bain Marie).

Princess of Wales

This nineteenth-century recipe shows in what high esteem milk was held as a cosmetic. Add the juice of a slice of lemon to half a pint of milk, and put it on your face at bedtime. Leave it on all night, and wash it off in the morning with lukewarm water. It is supposed both to freshen and nourish the skin.

Old Country Recipes for Elderflower Ointment

Takes 5 lb of lard and 1 lb of mutton suet and dissolve them in an earthenware pot. When they have melted add 5 pints of distilled elderflower water, remove from the heat and beat until the cream takes. The quantities here are enormous, so cut them down to suit your needs: say 2 oz lard, $\frac{1}{2}$ oz suet.

Using an enamel saucepan, melt 1 lb of lard. Then throw in 2 lb of fresh elderflowers. Simmer the mixture gently until the lard has taken on the scent of the elder blossoms.

Astringents

Pimpernel water, Plantain water, and Periwinkle water, described earlier, can all be used as mild astringents, as can Yarrow water, prepared in the same way.

Astringent for Dry, Sensitive Skin

Dry skin doesn't need a strong astringent, but something is often needed to remove cleansing cream, or just to freshen the face. The classic standby, rose water and glycerin, is the best for this kind of skin.

Yarrow. Pink or white, Yarrow flowers June–August and is found among grass

Mix three-quarters of rose water with one-quarter of glycerin. Orange flower water and glycerin can be used instead, or lavender water (non alcoholic) and glycerin.

Astringent for Oily Skin

A mixture of rose water and witch-hazel is good for oily skin – again, orange flower water or non-alcoholic lavender water can be substituted for the rose water.

These simple mixtures are very easy to make, much cheaper than many of the astringents available in the shops, and they work just as well.

Flowery Vinegar Astringent

Alcohol should only be used on oily skin, and then in very weak solution – no more than 20 per cent of a lotion, although old recipes recommend using white wine. Mrs Beeton suggests white wine in which leaves of crushed lemon balm have been steeped, and Master Alexis the Piedmontese, author of a medieval book of French beauty recipes says that rosemary steeped in white wine works well. Be that as it may, vinegar is gentler for dry and sensitive skin, and helps to restore its acid balance.

Here is a recipe: Steep in about four fluid ounces of white wine vinegar as much lavender, scented geranium leaves (which are astringent, as well as scented), and lemon balm leaves as the vinegar will cover. Add a few allspice berries. Place in a sealed jar, and leave for a week to infuse, shaking it vigorously every day. Strain, and add four ounces of orange flower water. If you like you can add a drop or two of geranium oil.

Pennyroyal Vinegar

Bruise one ounce of fresh pennyroyal leaves, put them in a jar, cover with white wine vinegar and leave it to infuse, covered, for one week. Shake the mixture daily, and then strain and bottle for use. Culpeper says that this vinegar 'takes away the marks of bruises and blows about the eyes, and burns in the face … '

A Victorian Water to Preserve the Colour of the Skin

Add a wine glass full of lemon juice to a pint of rain water, and five drops of rose water. The mixture should be kept well corked, and used only from time to time.

Face Masks

Face Mask to Feed Dry Skin

Although face masks can be used for every purpose, if you have dry skin it is probably better to avoid the deep cleansing masks, as they can be drying. Clean the face instead with a herbal steaming mixture, and then apply the following mask to feed and moisturise the skin.

2 tablespoons honey
1 tablespoon lanolin
1 tablespoon fuller's earth
1 egg yolk
apple juice: enough to mix to a suitable consistency

Mix to a paste and apply evenly to the face and neck.

Real apple juice must be used: grate three apples on a cheese grater, and squeeze the juice through a muslin cloth. Use more apples if necessary.

Rinse off after about 15 minutes with tepid water, and finish off with rose water and glycerin.

Stimulating and Tightening Mask

1 tablespoon honey
2 egg whites, whipped
1 tablespoon fuller's earth
mint tea – strong infusion – half a cup of dried mint to one cup of water
2 or 3 drops peppermint oil

Mix to a paste.

Add enough mint tea to make it the right consistency, and leave it on face and neck until it begins to set. Rinse off with tepid water, and use a gentle astringent, or even a cream if you have dry skin.

Peppermint Mask suitable for Dry Skin

Make a mucilage of agar agar following the instructions on the packet, but substituting a strong infusion of mint leaves for the water. A mucilage of Irish moss or of quince seeds can be used instead. Add 2 or 3 drops of essential oil of peppermint, and wait for the liquid to turn to a jelly. A little glycerin can be added before it sets if liked. Apply to the face for a few minutes and rinse off with tepid water. Follow it with a moisturiser or gentle astringent.

Mask to Remove Dead Skin, and Brighten the Complexion

Mix the juice of a lemon and the juice of a tomato with an equal quantity of almond oil. Put it all over your face, wet your hands, and slowly massage the skin. Rinse off with tepid water, and clean off the oil thoroughly with an astringent.

Almond

Deep Cleansing Mask for Oily Skin

This mask not only cleanses the skin, but tightens the pores, so if you have dry or sensitive skin with small pores, don't use it.

4 tablespoons fuller's earth
1 tablespoon lanolin
2 teaspoons agar agar powder (Irish moss or quince seeds can be substituted if liked)
A strong decoction of liquorice sticks (made by simmering them in enough water to cover them for half an hour in a covered pan: enough to mix to a paste. (Use four liquorice sticks.)

Mix all the ingredients to a paste, and apply to the face. Allow the mask to set slightly, then rinse off thoroughly with tepid water, and apply either moisturiser or astringent.

Almond and Honey Mask for the Bath

Mix 6 oz of ground almonds with 2 tablespoons of liquid honey and enough rose water to make a paste. Apply it to face and neck in the bath, and leave on for fifteen minutes. Rinse off.

Benzoin

'So weeps the wounded Balsome: so
The holy Frankincense doth flow.
The brotherless Heliades
Melt in such Amber Tears as these.'
Andrew Marvell.

Gum benzoin, balsam, or benjamin, as it is called in the old herbals, is a scented gum which has been used in cosmetics for hundreds of years. The benzoin tree, which grows in Thailand, Java and Sumatra, produces the gum only when it is wounded, and it solidifies into 'tears' when it meets the air.

The story of the 'brotherless Heliades' comes from Ovid's *Metamorphoses*: they were the daughters of the sun god, Helios, and the sisters of Phaeton, who drove the sun god's chariot, and, losing control, tumbled into the sea to an untimely death. The mourning Heliades were turned into trees but continued to weep for their brother. Their tears were turned into amber by the sun.

One of the cosmetics made with benzoin is Virgin-milk, which, along with Angelic Water, Celestial Water, and Venice Water was once as common as rose water is now.

Virgin Milk

Pour a few drops of simple tincture of benzoin (the compound tincture is Friar's Balsam, and not suitable), into a glass of rain water, or distilled water. Alternatively, add a few drops of essential oil of benzoin to half a cupful of alcohol-based lavender water, or Ethyl alcohol, and add a little of that to the water. This produces a milky liquid, whence its name. The 'Lady's Toilette' says, 'This virgin-milk, if the face be washed with it, will give a beautiful rosy colour ... it will render the skin clear and brilliant', if left to dry on the skin.

Benzoin is antiseptic, and is good for chapped and irritated skin. It was said in the nineteenth century that its scent produced a dreamy state of mind.

Benzoin

Schnouda – The Rouge of the 'Arabian Nights'

The legendary rouge of the *Arabian Nights*, which brings a natural blush to the cheeks, was made of benzoin and pommade of jasmine.

True pommade of jasmine is hard to make, and requires large quantities of fresh flowers, but here are two easier ways to achieve the same effect.

1 teaspoon white beeswax
1 tablespoon lanolin
3 tablespoons almond oil
1 tablespoon rose water
2½ teaspoons of essential oil of benzoin
5 drops of essential oil of jasmine

Follow the instructions given for making creams on page 18 (Bain Marie). Apply it to the cheeks as you would an ordinary rouge, and wait to see the results.

Or:

4 tablespoons clarified lard
2½ teaspoons of essential oil of benzoin
5 drops of essential oil of jasmine

Most cooking lard has already been purified, but, when you heat the lard, if any scum or froth should rise to the surface, skim it off. Add the oil of benzoin and the jasmine as the lard begins to cool, stir them in and pour it into a jar.

If you have simple tincture of benzoin instead of the essential oil, use less rose water and more tincture of benzoin.

Benzoin, which is the blush-producing ingredient in Schnouda, has more effect on some types of skin than it does on others. If the cream doesn't produce the desired result, you could try adding more benzoin until you find the strength that suits your skin.

Make-Up

Although the Chinese had only a limited number of perfumes, of which musk was their favourite, they did have quite elaborate cosmetics. Before retiring they would cover their faces with a mixture of rice flour and tea-oil, which they scraped off in the morning before applying a white powder called 'Meen Fun'. They rouged not only their cheeks, but their nostrils and the tips of their tongues, and finished up with a powder of ground rice.

Victorian ladies rouged the lobes of their ears, and their nostrils, a habit which their critics said made them look like rocking horses!

Medieval Face Powder

In the Middle Ages the only known face powder was powdered wheat. Either sift brown flour through a hair sieve, or grind some wheat in the mixer, and then pass it through the sieve. Although it doesn't sound very efficient, it makes a fine translucent powder. You can add a little powdered cinnamon, or orris root and orange peel for scent and warmth of colour. Brown flour gives a better colour. Orris can cause an allergic reaction, so experiment on a small patch of skin, preferably hidden by your hair.

Ancient Greek Rouge

The ancient Greeks used alkanet root as rouge: here is a modern version.

1 teaspoon white beeswax
3 tablespoons almond oil
1 tablespoon cocoa butter
2 teaspoons of powdered alkanet root
1 tablespoon rose water

Heat the alkanet with the almond oil in an enamel pan until the colour is well infused. Strain it. Melt the wax and the cocoa butter in the Bain Marie (see page 18) and add the coloured oil to them. Remove from the heat, and slowly add the rose water, beating until cold, as you would for ordinary cream.

Chinese Rouge

Extract the juice of a beetroot, and use it as rouge.

Lipstick

1 tablespoon Vaseline

1 teaspoon white beeswax
5 drops of red cochineal food colouring

Melt the wax and the Vaseline in a Bain Marie (see page 18). Remove from the heat and allow it to get quite cool, but not set hard. The colouring will not mix with the other ingredients if they are too hot or too cold. Stir in the cochineal, and pour the mixture into an old lipstick container. Place in the deep freeze compartment of your fridge until set.

This makes a good wine-coloured lipgloss.

To Darken the Eyebrows

An old way of darkening the eyebrows, which can only be done in the autumn, is to stain them with the juice of elderberries. Make several applications.

Rice Powder

'Take a new earthenware pot and fill it with six quarts of water and 2½ lbs of rice; leave the rice to soak for twenty-four hours, and then pour the water off. Put the same quantity of water over the rice for three days running. After the three immersions, each lasting twenty-four hours, drain the rice over a new hair-sieve kept for the purpose. Expose it to the air in a safe place, on a clean white cloth. As soon as it is dry, pound it quite fine with a pestle in a very clean mortar with a cover. Then strain it through a fine white cloth placed carefully over the pot which is to hold it, and which ought to be provided with a tight-fitting cover. This powder is better without perfume.' Baroness Staffe, *Lady's Dressing Room*, 1892.

You can use a coffee grinder or some kinds of mixer to powder the rice, instead of a pestle and mortar. You may disagree about the perfume, so if you want to scent it, add a few drops of essential oil to the powder, and re-sift it, making sure it is well mixed in. The powder will develop an even scent after a few days in a closed container. A mixture of brown and white rice can be used, and the colour can be altered by adding various powdered herbs. Hibiscus flowers (the flowers can be bought as tea from some health food shops) will make it pinker, orris root will make it a creamier colour, and give it a delicate scent, but be careful, because some people develop allergies to it. A little cinnamon will add warmth.

You can scent it with whatever you like: with vanilla, like Anne of Austria, wife of Louis XIII of France, which can be done by placing the powder in a jar with some vanilla pods for a week or two, or with oil of geranium, lavender, chamomile or rose.

The Body

The Baths of Ancient Rome

Although the Egyptians and the Greeks bathed and scented themselves with perfumed unguents, the custom reached its height amongst the Romans, and has never been rivalled since. Their baths were housed in buildings the size of palaces, lined with marble and mosaics, and surrounded by promenades of shady trees. They were the meeting place of the people of Rome, and the centre of social life. Inside were libraries and galleries of sculpture, as well as the baths themselves.

On arriving, the bather first entered the cold bath, or Frigidarium, then went on to the Tepidarium, and lastly entered the hot bath, or Caldarium, where he scrubbed himself with a type of bronze curry comb, and dropped scented oils on to the body. The whole procedure ended with a splash of cold water over the head.

It is obviously impossible to simulate the true Roman bath at home, but it is easy to go through the same process, taking a cold bath, then a tepid one, finishing off with a hot one, and a cold shower if you can face it! Substitute a loofah for the bronze curry comb, which would be painful and rather hard to come by, and anoint yourself with one of the oils or unguents mentioned below.

The rose was one of the favourite scents of the ancient Romans; the Emperor Heliogabalus bathed in wine of roses, and the floors of the rich were strewn with their petals.

Rose Unguent or Rhodium

4 tablespoons of cocoa butter
2 tablespoons of lard
2 tablespoons of rose water
3 teaspoons of essential oil of roses

Women's baths in Pompeii

Melt the lard and cocoa butter in a Bain Marie (see page 18), remove them from the heat, and beat in the rose water, adding it drop by drop. Finally add the essential oil of roses.

The other scents beloved by the Romans were calamus, or sweet rush, saffron, myrrh, spikenard, narcissus and quince blossom. The most famous of all was a lily unguent called Susinum, made from the lilies of Susa and from cinnamon, sweet rush, myrrh, and saffron. Many of these things, unfortunately, are not obtainable, but you can make a scented oil or an unguent from those that are.

Follow the instructions for the rose unguent, but instead of the essence of roses add a few drops of essential oil of myrrh, narcissus and cinnamon. Make a tincture of saffron by macerating a small amount in enough Ethyl alcohol to cover it; seal the container, and leave for 10 days in a warm place, shaking it every day. Strain. Beat the ingredients into the unguent, or if you prefer, an oil base can be used instead.

More Luxurious Baths

The Milk Bath

Cleopatra, Nero's wife Poppaea, and countless others, have bathed in milk. It was the height of fashion at the court of Charles II. Although it is cheaper than bathing in wine, as Mary Queen of Scots did, it is still a luxury that few can afford.

The Bath of Modesty

This is said to possess the same qualities as a bath of asses' milk, which softens and beautifies the skin, and is made as follows:

Marsh Mallow

'Take four ounces of pine-apple kernels, and one pound of elecampane, ten handfuls of linseed, one ounce of roots of marsh-mallows, and one ounce of lily-roots. Pound all these substances, make them into a paste, and tie it up in three little bags. Throw them into the water of the bath, and empty them by compression.'

Mme Tallier's Bath

Mme Tallier, one of Marie Antoinette's ladies-in-waiting, bathed herself in the juice of strawberries and raspberries. After the bath she was gently rubbed with sponges soaked in milk and delicate perfumes. Although extravagant, both strawberries and raspberries are extremely beneficial for oily skin, being astringent and stimulating, and, no doubt, imparting a faint pink to the skin as well.

Ninon de l'Enclos's Bath

Dissolve 3½ oz of carbonate of soda and 8 oz of salt in two pints of water. Dissolve 3 lb of honey in 6 pints of milk. Pour in the salt solution, and mix well. Then pour in the milk and honey and mix again.

Ninon de l'Enclos also used houseleek, thyme, rosemary, lavender and roses in her bath to preserve her beauty.

Bath Oils

'Huiles Antiques'

The oldest way of making scented oils is to fill a glass jar with fresh herbs or flowers, cover them with oil, and seal the jar. Place it in the sun for a week or so, then strain the oil. If it isn't strong

Bath time in Rome

enough, fill the oil with fresh flowers, and repeat the process until the oil is heavily scented. You can do this with any strongly scented or aromatic plant: roses, gardenias, honeysuckle, orange blossom, or with lavender, thyme, or basil. The oils mentioned below can be used for this method also.

Bath Oils using Essential Oils

These are extremely easy and cheap to make. You can use any of the following oils as a base: almond oil, sunflower seed oil, sesame oil, avocado oil, apricot kernel oil and many others. Don't use mineral oils; cold-pressed vegetable oils are better for the skin. Whichever oil you choose, add 5 or 10 per cent wheatgerm oil to it, as it will help preserve your bath oil, as well as feeding the skin with vitamin E. More than that, however, will disguise the scent.

For a dispersing bath oil, which is more like a commercial bath essence, use Turkey Red oil.

Essential Oils

These are available from some herbalists and perfumers, or by mail order from various stockists (see list on page 16), but they vary a lot, so shop around. If you aren't sure of their quality, stick to the fresh-smelling scents like lavender, bergamot, citronella or orange flower, as the delicate ones such as violet, lily or apple blossom can smell cloying and synthetic. If in doubt add a few drops of clary sage to your mixture; it is supposed to remove the synthetic smell.

When you have chosen the oil base you want, simply add a few drops of the essential oil, or oils, until you have achieved the strength of perfume you require.

Tropical Bath Oil

For the scent of the South Seas try a mixture of gardenia, lemongrass and ylang ylang, or of lemongrass and vanilla, which perfumes the air in Tahiti. Pour the essential oils, drop by drop, into the oil base and shake thoroughly.

The ylang ylang, or perfume tree, is a native of Mauritius and of the Philippines, where the women dress their hair with ylang ylang scented coconut oil. You probably will not want to follow their example, but it makes a nice ointment to rub on the body after the bath. In colder climates coconut oil remains solidified until applied to the body.

Frangipani is another scent of the Tropics. It is made from the sweet-smelling blossoms of the frangipani tree; the flowers grow from bare, silvery branches. Frangipani was the botanist who sailed to the West Indies with Columbus, and the scent

Columbus lands at San Salvador, 1492

of the frangipani tree, named after him, was the first intimation that land was near after their long voyage.

Another flower that grows freely in the South Seas is the hibiscus. Although it has no scent, it will colour your bath a deep pink: place one ounce of dried hibiscus flowers in a muslin bath bag,* and tie it under the hot water tap when your bath is running.

Mediterranean Bath Oil

The scents most evocative of the Mediterranean are lavender, mimosa, orange blossom, or neroli, petitgrain, made from the crushed leaves of orange and lemon trees, bergamot, tuberose, the 'mistress of the night', and jasmine. A good mixture is orange flower, citronella and bergamot; or try jasmine, rose and petitgrain, mimosa, or lavender and bay.

If you go to the Mediterranean, you can make a 'huile antique' by steeping relays of aromatic flowers and leaves in oil – for instance lavender, rosemary, orange and lemon leaves, scented geraniums, lemon verbena, wild thyme, and cistus. Both the garden and the wild varieties have a sticky substance on their leaves called galbanum which has a delicious scent (this gum used to be collected by driving herds of goats amongst the plants – the gum stuck to their beards, and was removed afterwards!).

Indian Bath Oil

Try a mixture of two parts jasmine called 'Moonlight of the Grove' by the Indians, and two parts

* Sew a bag out of doubled muslin and run a draw string around the top.

Frankincense

sandalwood to one part rose and half each of patchouli and cinnamon. Pour the essential oils into the oil of your choice, drop by drop, and shake the mixture thoroughly.

Biblical Bath Oil

The perfumes most often mentioned in the Bible are cedarwood, myrrh, hyssop, frankincense and lilies. Although strange, these scents are worth trying.

These mixtures are only suggestions – you can use just one scent in the oil or follow the recipes for scents in the chapter on scent, although they will not smell quite the same mixed with oil, or invent some of your own combinations.

Herbs and Flowers in the Bath

One of the most beneficial treatments for the skin is to bathe in flowers and herbs. Although it is more romantic to lie in a sea of scented petals, it is not so good when it comes to cleaning the bath afterwards. Buy a bath bag, or make one from doubled muslin with a draw-string round the top, fill it with the herbs of your choice, and tie it to the hot bath tap, allowing the water to run through it. When the bath is run, use the bag like a loofah.

Elecampane, Mint and Roses

Elecampane, once grown in every garden, and familiar to the Anglo-Saxon herbalists, was said to have sprung from the tears of Helen of Troy, and to be named after her, because she was carrying an armful of it when Paris abducted her.

Mint, named after the Greek nymph, Mentha, is one of the most refreshing and stimulating herbs for a summer bath, and it softens the skin.

Roses, surprisingly, are antiseptic. They are soothing to mind and body, as well as a tonic to the skin. They are used in aromatherapy to cure nausea, and for troubles of the womb.

You can put almost any herb or flower into your bathwater, as long as it is used in medicine or cosmetics and isn't poisonous. For example lavender, lemon balm, vervain, lime blossom, lovage as a deodorant, lupins, marigolds, jasmine, houseleek, hyssop, daisies, carnations, clover, nettles, comfrey, meadowsweet and St John's Wort.

'Take the Flowers or Peels of Citrons, the Flowers of Oranges and Jessamine (jasmine), Lavender, Hysop, Bay-Leaves, the Flowers of Rosemary, Comfry, and the Seeds of Coriander, Endive and sweet Marjoram; the Berries of Myrtle and Juniper; boil them in Spring-Water, after they are bruised, till a third part of the liquid Matter is consumed, and enter it in a Bathing-tub, or wash yourself with it warm, as you see Occasion, and it will indifferently serve for Beauty and Health.' Shirley, in *A Chaplet of Herbs.*

'Take Rosemary, Fetherfew, Orgaine, Pellitory of the Wall, Fennell, Mallowes, Violet-leaves, and Nettles, boyle all these together, and when it is well sodden put to it two or three gallons of milke; then let the Party stand or sit in it an houre or two, and when they come out they must go to bed and beware of taking cold.'

'A generall bath for clearing the skin and comforting the body', from *A Chaplet of Herbs.*

High Summer Bath

Take two handfuls each of hollyhock flowers, which are emollient, roses, which are soothing and also antiseptic, and lime blossom, which is the most calming of all the flowers, and soothing and healing to the skin.

Wrap the lime blossoms in a muslin bag (see above), and tie it under the hot tap as you run your bath. Scatter the rose petals and hollyhocks – as many colours as you can find – into the water. The bath will smell at first of lime blossom, but will slowly take on the scent of roses. It looks so pretty that it's worth having the flowers loose for this one.

The Wars of the Roses

Throw as many whole red, and white, roses into your bath as you can spare from your garden, minus their thorns! This bath has more than poetry; 'The Rose', according to the Greek poet Anacreon, 'distils a healing balm, the beating pulse of pain to calm', and is beneficial for any redness of the skin, and for the womb; it is antiseptic, and cheers the heart.

Summer Bath

Cooling, calming and refreshing: take two handfuls each of fresh lavender flowers, fresh mint, and the leaves and flowers of fresh hyssop. Tie them in a muslin bag (see page 46) and hang it from the hot water tap while the bath is running. These herbs, apart from their delicious fresh scent, are antiseptic, stimulating, cleansing and soothing to the skin.

A Bath for Aches and Pains

Refreshing and restorative: take two handfuls each of fresh, bruised bay leaves, which help rheumatism, vine leaves, which are restorative, and rose geranium leaves, which are astringent and delicious smelling, and one handful of crushed juniper berries, which are also good for rheumatism. Follow the instructions on page 46.

Cottage Garden Bath

Take two handfuls each of fresh meadowsweet, marigold petals, mignonette and lovage, and tie

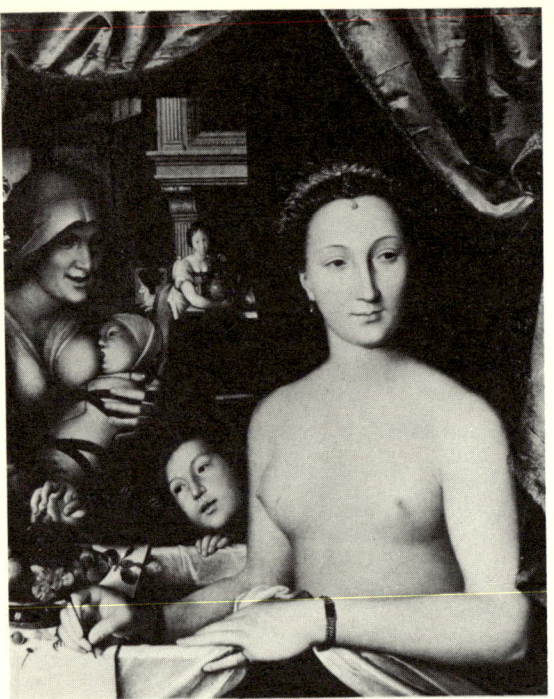

Diane de Poitiers, who became mistress of both Francis I and Henry II of France

Marie Antoinette's Bath

While Marie Antoinette was still Dauphine, she used to bathe herself in a decoction of serpolet (wild thyme), bay leaves, thyme and marjoram, to which a little sea salt had been added. Take two ounces each of all the herbs, place them in an enamel saucepan, cover with water, and bring to the boil. Allow to simmer for ten minutes, then infuse, covered, until cold. Add a cupful of salt and the strained decoction to the bath.

Diane de Poitiers

She used to bathe every morning in rain water, and walked frequently in the rain to preserve her complexion.

The Bath of Charles V of France

While staying at the monastery of St Yuste, Charles V, it is said, bathed himself daily in a water which contained lemon balm. He believed it sharpened his wits.

them in a muslin bag. Hang the bag from the hot water tap while the bath is running, then, if you want, use it to wash your skin.

Herbal Deodorants ...

A strong decoction, or infusion of any fresh smelling herb can be used as a deodorant, but lovage, thyme, and oak leaves are the most effective. Add them to any of the bath mixtures above, or use a strong infusion to splash yourself with.

Massage Oils

The ancient world was well aware of the therapeutic value of scented flowers and herbs. Pliny wrote about them, and Hippocrates used them to treat both physical and nervous disorders, as does modern aromatherapy. The sweet scent alone is considered beneficial in many cases. A massage with scented oils is one of the pleasantest and most effective ways of benefiting from them, and one of the most relaxing.

You can make massage oils by adding essential oils to any of the following oils: almond, peach kernel, apricot kernel, avocado. Any vegetable oil will do, but these are the nicest and best for the skin. Massage oils differ from bath oils only in being less strongly scented, and it is more important to be sure that the essential oils you use are the real thing, or you won't get so much benefit from them. (The Aromatic Oil Company, 12 Littlegate Street, Oxford, sell essential oils especially for aromatherapy.)

Always add 10 per cent wheatgerm oil to the oil of your choice, as this will prevent the mixture from oxidising too quickly.

A Relaxing Massage Oil

Add two or three drops each of rose oil and sandalwood oil to 8 fluid ounces of peach kernel oil and one of wheatgerm oil. The contents of four vitamin E capsules can be added for greater benefit to the skin, and to help preserve the oil. This oil is quite heavy and sensuous, but if you prefer something with a lighter scent, try substituting chamomile and lavender for the rose and sandalwood.

An Invigorating and Refreshing Massage Oil

Add two drops each of peppermint oil, rosemary oil and bergamot, and one of lavender to 8 fluid ounces of almond oil and one ounce of wheatgerm oil. Shake the bottle well. (Some people are allergic to bergamot, so experiment.)

Charles V of France

For Rough Skin and for the Neck

Paste of the Scythian Women

Herodotus tells us that the women of Scythia made their bodies soft and scented by using a paste made in the following way: bruise chippings of cedarwood, cypress wood and frankincense in a pestle and mortar (they did it with a stone), and add enough water to make a paste. Cover your body with it and leave it for a while before washing off with warm water. It leaves the skin slightly scented and soft.

Another, more modern version can be made by adding a few drops of essential oils of cypress, cedarwood and frankincense (which is olibanum), to a mucilage of agar agar or quince seeds, and then adding one quarter as much glycerin, and shaking well.

Rough Skin Lotion

4 tablespoons of avocado oil
1 tablespoon of strong comfrey leaf infusion
1 tablespoon of strong infusion of sweet woodruff
1 pinch of borax
6 vitamin E capsules (contents of)

Heat the avocado oil in a china basin suspended over a saucepan of boiling water until it has become quite runny. Remove the basin from the heat and slowly add the comfrey and woodruff in which the borax has been dissolved, beating all the time. Add the vitamin E, and continue beating until the ingredients are well mixed.

Neck Cream

The neck is always supposed to reveal age more than any other part of the body, so it is important to use a good neck cream: this one contains ginseng and sandalwood, both famous for their rejuvenating qualities, and cocoa butter, which is supposed to have a particularly beneficial effect on the lines of the neck.

2 tablespoons cocoa butter (oil of theobroma)
6 tablespoons almond oil
2 tablespoons ginseng elixir (liquid form)
6 vitamin E capsules (contents of) (also rejuvenating)
a few drops of essential oil of sandalwood
1 teaspoon white beeswax

Follow the instructions given on page 18 (Bain Marie).

The Sun

Different parts of the world produce different oils, and it is probably better to use the local one: coconut oil in the West Indies and the Pacific, olive oil in the Mediterranean.

Sun Oil for the Tropics

Add a few drops of essential oil of ylang ylang, sometimes called the 'perfume tree', to a jar of coconut oil: if you are making it on the spot the oil will probably be liquid, but in colder countries it will have solidified, so melt it gently in a Bain Marie (see page 18) before adding the scent. The women of the Philippines use it to anoint their hair, but it makes a lovely sun oil.

AGAINST INSECTS: substitute oil of citronella for the ylang ylang to discourage sandflies, and for scent, add a couple of drops of vanilla oil, a product of the Pacific islands, which the famous perfumer Septimus Piesse, inventor of the musical scale of perfumes, considered to be the natural complement of citronella. A more solid version can be made by using two-thirds coconut oil to one-third cocoa butter: melt them together in the Bain Marie before adding the essential oil, then pour into a screw-top jar, not a bottle.

Mediterranean Sun Oil

Olive oil is a wonderful sun oil. Add a few drops of essential oil of bergamot, which has a lovely scent, and encourages tanning. Experiment with a small amount first, as some people develop allergies to bergamot. If you do, use neroli oil (orange flower), instead, which smells of the Mediterranean, and is soothing to the skin.

After-Sun Lotions to soothe Sunburn

The simplest, and probably the most readily available cure for burning skin is, I am told, to bathe in a lukewarm bath full of seaweed! However, you may not feel much like it after a long day at the beach, so take the following lotion with you:

Agar Agar, Witch-Hazel and Comfrey Lotion

Make up a mucilage of agar agar, following the instructions on the packet, but substitute equal quantities of witch-hazel and a strong infusion of comfrey leaves for the water. Scent with geranium oil, which also soothes burns. Keep in the fridge if the weather is very hot, or add a chemical preservative. Irish moss or quince seeds can be used instead of agar agar.

Elderflower Water and Glycerin

Follow the instructions on page 19 for distilling elderflowers. They are healing and soothing to the skin. Mix two-thirds elderflower water to one part glycerin, and shake the bottle thoroughly, or use it on its own as an *eau de toilette*.

Anti-Mosquito Splash

Add a couple of small drops of oil of citronella to a bottle of witch-hazel, or a bottle of orange flower water, and shake the bottle.

Pregnancy

As it is impossible to get rid of stretch marks once you have them, it is essential to use a good

Bladderwrack

oil on breasts and stomach before the marks appear.

Anti-Stretch-Mark Oil

2 tablespoons cocoa butter
3 tablespoons wheatgerm oil
6 vitamin E capsules (contents of)
a few drops of essential oil of chamomile (strengthens the tissues)

Melt the cocoa butter in a china basin suspended over a saucepan of boiling water, remove from the heat, and add the other ingredients.

Any oil will give elasticity to the skin, but this mixture should give it the best chance. It must be used every night before going to bed, and massaged in.

For the Breasts – Lady's Mantle

4 tablespoons wheatgerm oil
1 teaspoon white beeswax
1 pinch borax
4 vitamin E capsules (contents of)
2 tablespoons of a strong infusion of the whole plant of lady's mantle (*Alchemilla vulgaris*) which should be gathered when in full flower.

To make, follow the instructions on page 18 (Bain Marie).

Lady's mantle has a reputation for firming the breasts; according to both Gerard and Culpeper, who says it 'helps ... women who have over flagging breasts, causing them to grow less and hard, both when drank and outwardly applied ... '

'The Mother',
from a group by J. H. Foley

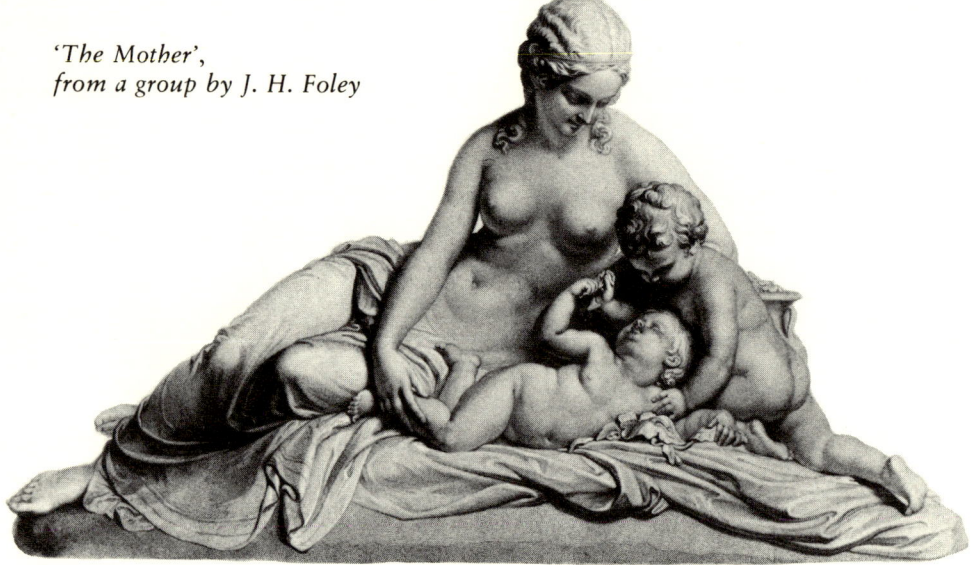

He also said it encourages conception if the distilled water is 'drank for twenty days together'.

Geoffrey Grigson suggests that its name, *Alchemilla*, means 'little alchemical one', and it has always been considered a magical and powerful plant, as it catches the much-prized morning dew like diamonds in its leaves.

Talcum Powder

Lots of different things can be used instead of ordinary talcum powder: any sweet or fresh scented flower can be powdered once dry, and mixed with others to make a delicious powder, which is also good for the skin. You can use unscented talcum powder as the base, or kaolin, but you will need one or the other to keep the powder pale. The paler the flowers you choose, the more you can use in proportion to the powder base.

Orange Blossom and Jasmine Powder

1 oz jasmine flowers, dried
1 oz orange flowers, dried
2 oz kaolin, or unscented talc

Reduce the flowers to a fine powder in a coffee grinder, and pass them through a fine sieve. Add them to the talcum powder or kaolin, and sieve again. Put the mixture in a sealed container, and let the scent develop for a week or two; it should grow stronger as the scents mingle and interact.

Lavender and Orris Powder

1 oz lavender flowers, dried
1 oz orris root, powdered
2 oz kaolin, or unscented talc

Applying powder, eighteenth-century style

Some people are allergic to orris, so if you are, leave it out. Powder the dried lavender flowers in a coffee grinder, and pass them through a fine sieve. Add them to the powder base, and sift again. Keep in a sealed container for two weeks before using.

Pink Powder

2 oz strongly scented pink rose petals
  (old fashioned roses smell more)
2 oz pinks
1 oz orris root, powdered
2 oz unscented talc

Choose pinks and roses that are as close to shell pink as you can find. If you are gathering them yourself, be sure to use only the petals. Dry them according to the pot pourri method on page 99.

Once the petals are dry, powder them in a coffee grinder, add the orris root unless you have an allergy to it, grind once more, and sift through a fine sieve. Leave in sealed jar for two weeks before using.

New-Mown Hay Powder

1 oz tonquin beans
1 oz chamomile flowers
4 oz kaolin, or unscented talc

Powder the chamomile flowers in a coffee grinder, pass them through a fine sieve and add them to the powder or kaolin. Put through a sieve again, and place in a sealed container with the whole, dried tonquin beans amongst it. Leave the mixture for two or three weeks, shaking it gently from time to time, and when the scent is strong enough, remove the tonquin beans.

You can use most scented flowers, but many of them tend to be too dark. Lime blossom smells very good, marigolds are healing to the skin, lemon peel adds freshness, calamus smells wonderful. Essential oils can also be added, but resift the powder after the oils have dried in, to make sure that it all mixes together.

Almond Paste, or Hemsia

The beauties of the French court, under Louis XIII and Anne of Austria, whitened their hands and

Anne of Austria

shoulders with pastes from Spain, made from almonds and vanilla. Anne of Austria's skin was so delicate that Cardinal Mazarin used to tell her that, if she went to hell, her punishment would be to sleep in Holland sheets. Almonds are softening and bleaching to the skin, and so cleansing that they can be used instead of soap. Arab women make an almond soap called Hemsia.

Almond Paste

4 oz ground almonds
8 fl. oz triple rose water
4 fl. oz Ethyl alcohol
3 drops essence of vanilla, or almond essence

Soak the almonds in the rose water for an hour, then transfer to an enamel saucepan and boil some of the liquid away – the paste should be firm once it has dried. Add the alcohol while straining through a hair sieve. Allow it to cool, then add the essence of vanilla or almond.

While in the bath apply a thick coating to neck and shoulders, massaging it into your skin, and then rinse off with warm water.

The *Lady's Toilette*, an anonymous work published in 1822, gives another recipe for almond paste, to white and soften the hands and arms:

Steep one pound of ground almonds for two or three hours in milk; strain through a linen rag, and squeeze hard. Put the filtered matter on the fire, and add half a pound of white bread, two drams of borax, and the same quantity of calcined alum; lastly, put in an ounce of spermaceti. Stir with a wooden spoon and cook as long as you think fit.

This recipe uses a pound of ground almonds, which, as the mixture will not keep very long, is more than you will need, so make as much as you want to use immediately. The spermaceti is not essential. None of these almond pastes keeps long, so make them as you want to use them.

Virgil tells us that if the almond tree is covered with blossom, a hot summer and a bountiful harvest will follow.

Soap

Making soap from scratch is rather complicated and can be dangerous, as it is usually very alkaline, and can even remove your skin, but plain soaps can be scented, or enriched with natural things like lanolin, honey and herbs. The best soaps to use are those made with olive oil – large, square blocks of French olive oil soap can be bought – or 'Simple Soap', which has no scent or colour added to it. The best of all is pure Castile soap, a very high grade of white olive oil soap, but it is very difficult to get.

Rich Moisturising Soap

2 cupfuls plain soap, grated
2 tablespoons honey
2 tablespoons lanolin
1 teaspoon essential oil of rose geranium
1 tablespoon rose water

Any other essential oil can be used instead. Grate the soap on a cheese grater, and put it in the china bowl Bain Marie described on page 18. Add the rose water, the honey and the lanolin. Allow the soap to melt completely, stirring from time to time. Place a piece of cling foil over any soap-shaped container so that the soap does not stick to the sides. Add the essential oil to the mixture, and pour it into the container. When the soap has solidified, remove from its box. It is now ready to use.

Honey and Lemon Soap

Honey is one of the best foods for the skin, and lemon is very cleansing, so this is a good mixture.

2 cupfuls plain soap, grated
¼ cup honey
1 teaspoonful essential oil of lemon

Follow instructions above.

Soft Herb Soap

This makes a soap of a jelly-like consistency, which is very nice to use. It should be kept in a jar.

2 tablespoons borax
1 oz rosemary
1 oz thyme
1 oz sage
1 oz lemon verbena, or lemon balm
1 cupful plain soap, grated
water (enough to cover the herbs)
Essential oils, of one or more of the herbs used – to your taste.

Place the herbs in an enamel saucepan, cover them with water, bring them to the boil with the lid on, remove from the heat and infuse, covered, until

Rosemary

cool. Strain. Grate the soap on a cheese grater, and put it in a china basin Bain Marie (see page 18). Dissolve the borax in the herbal infusion, and add it to the soap. Stir from time to time until the soap has completely melted. Add the essential oil.

This soap will not keep indefinitely owing to the large amount of infusion in it, so prolong its life by keeping it in a screw-top jar with the lid on.

Napoleon's Favourite Soap

This went by the unromantic name of 'Brown Windsor'; perhaps his desire to conquer England had something to do with it; and it was scented with cassia oil, a relation of cinnamon, and oils of rosemary, lavender, petitgrain, which comes from the leaves of the orange tree, bergamot, clove, caraway, and cedarwood. A little bit of castor and styrax were also added, but these are harder to come by, and it smells very nice without. It can be made by grating a pure white soap such as 'Simple Soap', melting it in a Bain Marie, and adding the essential oils. Pour it into a square wooden tray, or any container of a suitable size, having lined it first with kitchen foil to prevent it sticking.

'A Delicate Washing-Ball'

'Take three ounces of orace [powdered orris root], half an ounce of Cypres, two ounces of *Calamus Aromaticus*, one ounce of Rose leaves, two ounces of Lavender flowers: beat all these together in a mortar, searcing them thorow a fine Searce, then scrape some Castill sope [olive oil soap], and dissolve it with some Rose-water, then incorporate all your powders therewith, by labouring of them well in a mortar.'

From *Ram's Little Dodoen*, 1606

Napoleon Bonaparte

'To Make an Ipswich Ball'

'Take a pound of fine white Castill Sope [olive oil soap], shave it thin in a pinte of Rose-water, and let it stand two or three dayes, then pour all the water from it, and put to it half a pinte of fresh water, and so let it stand one whole day, then pour out that, and put half a pinte more, and let it stand a night more, then put to it half an ounce of powder called sweet Marjoram, a quarter of an ounce of powder of Winter Savoury, two or three drops of the oyl of Spike [lavender], and the Oil of Cloves, three grains of Musk, and as much Ambergris, work all these together in a fair Mortar, with the powder of an Almond Cake dryed, and beaten as small as fine flowre, so rowl it round in your hands in Rose-water.' From *The Queen's Closet Opened*, by W. M., Cook to Queen Henrietta Maria, 1655.

'A Delicate wash-ball'

'Take a quarter of a Pound of *Calamus aromaticus*, a quarter of a Pound of Lavender flowers, six ounces of Orris, two ounces of Rose leaves, and an ounce of Cypres; pownd all these together in a Mortar, and rub them through a fine Sieve, then scrape Castile-soap, and dissolve it in Rose-water, put in your beaten Powder, pownd it in a Mortar, and make it up into Balls.' From *The Receipt Book of John Nott*, Cook to the Duke of Bolton, 1723.

Hair

Shampoo

The word shampoo is of Hindu origin, and in eighteenth-century England it was used to describe the kind of massage you get in a Turkish bath. By the nineteenth century it had come to mean massaging and washing the scalp, which was a novel idea, and it met with great opposition from the doctors and beauty experts of the day. *Lady's Toilette*, a Victorian book on beauty, says: 'Look at those children whose heads are scarcely ever dry; their pallid faces will never be enlivened by the rich colours of adolescence, and the smiles of infancy will speedily be succeeded by the wrinkles of age.' It was an old adage that one should 'wash the hands often, the feet seldom, and the head never'. Instead, the hair should be kept clean with powdered bran or ivory powder, and brushed frequently with a clean brush.

Ideas have certainly changed, and I doubt if anyone will want to follow the example of our forebears on that score, but it is certainly true that too much shampooing does remove the natural oils, making dry hair more brittle and greasy hair greasier. Washing the hair-brush every day, as people used to do, keeps the hair clean longer, so it saves trouble in the end.

Different Ways of Making Shampoo

The easiest thing to do is to add a strong infusion of herbs to a good detergent shampoo, to give your hair extra gloss, manageability, and even colour. Many people believe, however, that hair should

Plaiting hair

never be washed with commercial detergent shampoos, as it strips it of its natural oils, making it necessary to replace them with artificial ones. Instead they recommend using a good olive oil soap, mixed with herbs, which cleans the hair thoroughly, but doesn't strip it of all its oils. It also makes the hair thicker, possibly because the alkalinity of soap causes each hair to retain more moisture, thus adding body.

The only drawback to a soap-based shampoo is that it tends to create scum in hard water, so if you live in a hard-water area it is better to stick to the detergents – the added herbs will do their job any way.

Lastly, for the real purists, a shampoo can be made without using either soap or detergent: soapwort root, which can be obtained from herbalists, produces a slight lather, and added to other herbs, makes a nice, light shampoo, but it certainly isn't as efficient as the other two methods.

If you want to use the first method, adding herbal infusions to detergent shampoo, use any of the herbal mixtures mentioned in the following recipes.

Shampoo for Weak Hair

This is an old recipe, using pure Castile soap, which is hard to get – any good olive oil soap will do instead, such as 'marseille pur', a French soap sold in rough, square blocks at some health food shops.

Pour a pint of boiling water over three ounces of grated soap, and keep the mixture at boiling point, without allowing it to cook, until the soap is completely melted. Pour into a jar, and allow it to set. When you want to use it, mix a tablespoonful with a raw egg and a pinch of bicarbonate of soda, and beat them together thoroughly. Rub it into the scalp and hair before using any water.

Hairdressing at home

Shampoo for all Types of Hair

To give extra shine, stimulate growth and help general condition.

1½ oz herbs: equal quantities of

rosemary
nettles
quassia chips
lime blossoms
1½ oz grated olive oil soap
¾ pint spring water or distilled water (tap water will do, but it isn't so good)
A few drops of essential oil of lavender

Place the herbs in an enamel saucepan and pour the water over them. Stir to mix. Bring to the boil, simmer gently for a minute or two, then remove from the heat and allow to infuse, covered, until the liquid is cool. Put the grated soap in a china basin suspended over a saucepan of boiling water on the stove, pour over it the strained infusion, and wait for the soap to melt, stirring occasionally. Pour into a bottle or jar

Rosemary, the herb of memory, is probably the best treatment you can give your hair; it makes it glossier, stimulates growth, reduces tangles, and even has a centuries-old reputation for preventing the fatal effects of rainy weather on curly hair.

Nettles, which spring up relentlessly wherever man makes his dwelling place, are regarded as a curse; but they are one of the best tonics for the blood in spring time, being rich in iron, and for the hair, as they stimulate its growth. They are, not surprisingly, ruled by Mars, but their warlike stings were not always thought to be evil: they protected their victims from the dangers of witchcraft.

Quassia chips add highlights to the hair, and are very cleansing.

Lime blossoms add gloss and soften the hair, making it more manageable.

Shampoo to Stimulate Growth

1½ oz herbs: equal quantities of

southernwood
yarrow
rosemary
sage for dark hair, or chamomile for blonde
1½ oz grated pure olive oil soap
¾ pint distilled water (or tap water)
A few drops of essential oil of bay

Follow the instructions, above, for shampoo for all types of hair.

Southernwood, or Lad's Love, with its strange, bitter scent has been grown in English gardens for centuries, and it is a powerful stimulant for the hair, encouraging growth and lustre.

Yarrow, one of the divinatory herbs, is a good astringent and conditioner for both hair and scalp.

Sage, rosemary and chamomile are the three most famous herbs for healthy, glossy hair: Sage is used as a rinse to cover grey hair, and is more suitable for dark hair, while chamomile conditions and adds highlights to light brown and blonde hair.

Peppermint Shampoo for Greasy Hair

1½ oz peppermint leaves
A few quassia chips
1½ oz grated pure olive oil soap
¾ pint distilled water (or tap water)
A few drops of essential oil of petitgrain

Place the quassia chips in an enamel saucepan and simmer, covered, for 10 minutes. Then follow the instructions above.

Peppermint leaves combat greasy hair, they are cleansing and gentle, and their fresh scent, combined with the oil of petitgrain, will leave your hair very pleasantly scented.

Oil of petitgrain is made from the leaves of the

orange tree, and has a clear, clean scent that is said to stimulate awareness; it is also good for greasy hair, as are quassia chips.

Quassia

Shampoo for Dry Hair

1½ oz herbs: equal quantities of
  comfrey leaf
  chamomile
  rosemary
  orange blossom
1½ oz grated pure olive oil soap
¾ pint distilled water
A few drops of essential oil of neroli.

Follow the instructions for making the shampoo above.

  Comfrey is a great healer, and soothes and enriches dry, lifeless hair; chamomile softens it, and will highlight blonde hair, and give a sheen to dark hair. Rosemary is a cure all for every type of hair. Oil of neroli is the essential oil obtained from orange blossoms, which moisturise dry hair; the oil from the leaves, called petitgrain, suits greasy hair, so it seems that the orange tree can provide all that is needed to maintain the balance of oils.

  This shampoo should be used as part of the general treatment for dry, brittle hair that follows; it really needs more than just a shampoo, and benefits greatly from massaging with oils.

Overhaul for Hair in Bad Condition

For dry, lustreless hair, split ends, and the effects of too much exposure to sun and sea water.

  Rub into your hair a mixture of almond oil, against dryness, and walnut oil, against split ends.

Wrap your head in a towel, turban-style, for several hours. Olive oil is very good too. Shampoo out using the shampoo for dry hair if your hair is very dry anyway, or using the greasy hair shampoo if not. Rinse with an infusion of rosemary, nettles, chamomile and orange blossom, pouring the liquid through your hair again and again for maximum effect.

Neutral Henna

If you want to dye your hair, use a coloured henna, or one of the henna mixtures in the section of hair dyes, but if you want to keep your natural colour, use neutral henna, or henna wax, which are probably the best hair conditioners you can find, and also help split ends.

Conditioning Rinses

After shampooing, it is a good idea to use a herbal rinse to help condition the hair.

Rinse to add Gloss, to encourage Growth, and make the Hair more manageable

Make a strong infusion of the following herbs: rosemary, nettles, maidenhair fern, and burdock root. Put the herbs in an enamel saucepan, cover with water (enough to rinse the hair), bring to the boil, allow it to simmer for a few minutes, then remove it from the heat and let it infuse until cool. Strain and use.

Rinse for Greasy Hair

Make a strong infusion, following the instructions above, of witch-hazel bark and rosemary, and scent with any essential oil you like.

Rinse for Dry Hair

Make a strong infusion of orange blossoms and chamomile flowers, and scent with either chamomile or neroli oil.

Tips for the Hair from Past and Present

Chinese women used to give lustre to their hair with pheasants' eggs – but the yolk of an ordinary hen's egg will do. Wet your hair with cool water and rub the yolk into the hair and scalp a few minutes before shampooing.

To Curl the Hair

A decoction of the roots of dwarf elder (not to be confused with ground elder, which is so common in gardens), is said to make the hair curl. It is also called Danewort, and was once thought to have sprung from the blood of the Danish invaders. It is a plant of St John's Eve, the real midsummer's eve which falls on the twenty-third of June, and so is best gathered on that day.

To Make it Grow

The hair should be cut only on the first day of the new moon – you then have two clear weeks ahead in which everything grows more freely – when the moon is on the wane, the life force in plants also ebbs away.

'An Ointment to make the Hair Grow'

'Take three spoonfuls of honey, and three handfuls of vine tendrils. Pound the latter well, and express the juice, which mix with the honey. Wash the parts with it where you wish the hair to grow long and thick'.

To Stop the Hair from Falling Out

This old remedy has the advantage of being very simple: powder your head with parlsey seeds three times a year, before going to bed, and your hair, it is said, will never fall out.

A Medieval Recipe to make the Hair Grow

'Take the barberry [a shrub with small yellow flowers in May and June, and red berries in autumn, growing in the hedgerows] and fill an iron pot therewith, fill it up with as much water as it will contain, then boil on a slow fire to half. With this water wash your head morning and evening. Take care that the wash does not touch any part where the hair should not grow.'

'The School of Salernum', an early source of cosmetic recipes, recommends southernwood, dill, the ashes of rats, moles and hedgehogs, to make the hair grow.

Nettles to make the Hair Grow

Comb your hair the wrong way every morning with the expressed juice of nettles.

Lemon Juice

The juice of a lemon added to the last rinse is

Lemon

helpful for both greasy hair and blonde hair, as it is a mild bleach when exposed to the sun.

Rosemary and Bay

A few drops of oil of bay or rosemary brushed through the hair every day will make it healthier and stronger.

Colour Rinses and Dyes

Red Hair and Golden Red Hair

There are many strange associations and prejudices attached to red hair, perhaps because it has never been common. Throughout the Middle Ages, because Judas was believed to have had red hair, it was considered a sign of treachery and unpredictability. Red is also the colour of Mars, and so the red-headed were supposed to have the fiery temper of the god of war.

As the Middle Ages drew to a close the evil reputation of red hair faded, and it became very fashionable in Venice, where the ladies tried to imitate the copper-coloured hair of Titian's goddesses (copper was the metal of Venus), or to achieve the pale reddish gold known as 'Capelli fila d'oro', the famous 'golden thread' hair of the Renaissance. It also became the fashion in Elizabethan England, where the queen herself had red hair.

The recipes in this section are for both red and golden hair because what our ancestors called golden, to us appears quite red, and the various dyes will, of course, create different effects on different coloured hair.

Here are some early recipes:

'To Make the Hair Red'

'Take of the water of radish and of privet as much as is sufficient; mix them well and wash the hair.'

'To Produce Golden Hair' (a reddish gold)

'Take the bark of rhubarb and infuse it in white wine; wash your head therewith, dry with a fine cloth, then by the fire or in the sun if it be warm. Do this once and again and the oftener you do it the more beautiful your hair will become, and that without injury to the hair.'

Rhubarb is ruled by Mars, according to Culpeper, as are radishes, used in the recipe above.

'... to make 'em Red, wash 'em with a decoction of Boxwood' Radcliffe.

Capelli Fila d'Oro

The Contessa Nani, who wrote the first Venetian book on cosmetics in the sixteenth century, gives another recipe for the 'golden thread hair' then so much admired. It consists of two pounds of alum, six ounces of black sulphur and four ounces of honey distilled with water. Even if black sulphur were easily available, I dread to think what it would do to the hair, so I don't recommend this one. The ladies of Venice, having applied this mixture to their hair, retired to their roof tops, and, wearing a crownless hat called a 'solana', allowed the sun many hours to bleach their tresses to the desired colour.

The sun certainly helps to bring out the colour with any of the golden, blonde, or reddish dyes.

Saffron Crocus

Saffron

'He hath slept in a bed of saffron' is an old expression to describe a man light of heart; saffron was famous for its exhilarating effects, and was also one of the dyes used to achieve 'golden thread hair'.

Add a small amount of boiling water to a few stamens of saffron, and allow it to infuse, covered, for several hours. Rinse through the hair repeatedly after shampooing.

Trotula of Salerno, a mythical figure in the world of beauty, left a recipe for reddish gold hair using saffron: it consists of equal parts of saffron, flowers of golden broom, elder bark, and the yolk of an egg beaten and boiled in water. A pommade gathers on the top of the mixture, which is skimmed off and used as a dye.

Henna

The flowers of henna give off a heady scent, which was much loved by Mohammed, but it is the powdered leaves which give the famous red dye. It is probably the most efficient method of obtaining red hair.

In the countries of its origin it is thought to possess mystical qualities; the red dye is seen as the life force of the earth, and its use connects mankind with it.

It can be used alone, or with other dye-yielding substances, and will have varying results depending on the original colour of your hair and the length of time it is left on. It is also one of the best conditioners.

To apply Henna

Put two or three ounces of henna, depending on the length of your hair, into a bowl, and mix to a

Other Dyes to mix with Henna

Crushed cloves can be mixed with henna for a browner effect, as can coffee grounds; lemon juice will increase its brightening qualities on mid brown hair; alkanet root, which yields a strong red dye, can be added to achieve a vivid red; chamomile and henna will give a golden red colour to pale brown hair.

Shampoo for Red Hair

This shampoo will add red highlights to hair that is already red.

1½ oz herbs: equal quantities of
   henna leaves
   marigold flowers
   chamomile flowers
   red hibiscus flowers
1½ oz grated pure olive oil soap
¾ pint distilled water
A few drops of essential oil of roses, or any other red flower.

Place the herbs in an enamel saucepan and bring to the boil. Allow to simmer gently for several minutes, then remove from the heat and let them infuse until cool. Follow the instructions for Shampoo for all types of hair on page 62 above.

Red Rinse to Follow

To get a stronger colour, make a strong infusion of the herbs used in the shampoo above, and rinse it through your hair again and again.

Marigold Hair Rinse – Virgin Mary Gold

Make a strong infusion of marigold flowers (about

paste with hot water. Wearing rubber gloves, part your wet, clean hair, apply the paste with a comb or brush, and make sure it covers all your hair. Pile it all up on top of your head, cover with a piece of silver baking foil and wash face and neck carefully to avoid dyeing them red also.

If you have very dark brown or black hair it should be left on for as long as possible, and will give dark auburn highlights.

The paler your hair, the redder it will go, so experiment every quarter of an hour by washing out a few strands and reapplying some new henna paste afterwards.

Rinse out, and shampoo.

two ounces in half a pint of water) and pour it through your hair again and again, catching the liquid in a bowl below. The word marigold comes from Mary's Gold, after the Virgin Mary, so it is suitable that it should also be a golden hair dye!

Strawberry Blonde

If you have blonde hair, you can get a bright shade of strawberry blonde by using powdered alkanet root, a dye known to the ancient Greeks.

Follow the instructions for 'Red Hair Shampoo', but substitute alkanet for the herbs. The powdered root should be simmered for at least half an hour to get its full colour, and the strained liquid added to the soap in the usual way.

Follow the shampoo with a rinse of the same decoction.

Blonde Hair

Chamomile makes blonde hair blonder, and brightens and highlights mouse and mid-brown. It has to be applied several times to get the full effect if used as a rinse, so don't lose heart.

There are several ways you can use it:

Chamomile Dye

1 oz quassia chips
2–3 oz powdered chamomile flowers, depending on length of hair.

Place the quassia chips, which help bring out the dye of the chamomile, in an enamel saucepan, and pour over them two cups of water. Bring to the boil, and simmer for half an hour. Strain off the water, and pour it over the powdered chamomile. Use only enough to make a thickish paste.

Apply the paste to clean, towel-dried hair, as you would for henna, making sure that all your hair is covered, and that the paste doesn't go on your face. Cover your hair, piled up on your head, in a bath cap, to keep your hair warm, and to prevent it drying.

It is really a matter of choice how long you want to leave the pack on your hair; it depends what colour it is in the first place, and how strong a colour you want to achieve. Rinse out with hot water.

This is the most effective way of using chamomile, as it is so much more concentrated, but you can also make a paste using one part kaolin powder to two parts of a strong chamomile infusion – bring the flowers and an equal quantity of water, or more, to the boil, remove from the heat, and allow to infuse until cool, then add the kaolin powder to the strained liquid, and proceed as above.

Chamomile, Marigold and Quassia Rinse

2 oz chamomile flowers
1 oz marigold flowers
½ oz quassia chips

Cover the quassia chips with 3 cupfuls of water in an enamel saucepan. Bring to the boil, and simmer for half an hour. Pour the strained liquid over the chamomile and marigold flowers, and allow them to infuse until cold. Strain, and pour over wet, shampooed hair, catching the rinse as it falls in a basin, and pouring it again and again.

'To turn the Hair yellow'

'A lye of the ashes of old Colworts, with shavings of the Box-tree, Liquorish, and Saffron; the Decoction of Broom-flowers also, and of the flowers of Mullein, do the same, as also Citron-Peels, Water and Oyl of Honey, and the like. These and such-like medicines are chiefly required whenas the Hair grows gray, or whenas the colour is meet to be changed into another.' Drage, in *A Chaplet of Herbs*.

These herbs, or many of them, are still used to make the hair blonde.

If you have blonde hair you are, it seems, in rather strange company; Baroness Staffe, in the *Lady's Dressing Room*, gives a list of famous blondes from history. It includes Eve, Venus, Lucretia Borgia, Catherine and Marie de' Medici, Anne of Austria, who scented all her cosmetics with vanilla, Madame de Sévigné, Marie Antoinette and the Empress Eugénie.

'To make the Hair fair and beautiful'

'Cleanse it from Dust, by washing it in Rose-Vinegar (made by steeping rose petals in white wine vinegar), then boil an Ounce of Turmerick, the like quantity of Rhubarb, with the leaves of Bay-Tree cut small, to the Quantity of a handful, boiled in a Quart of Water, wherein half a Pound of Allum has been dissolved; and by often washing your Head with the Decoction, it will make your Hair fair and lovely, unless it be a deep Red or exceeding Black.' Shirley, in *A Chaplet of Herbs*.

Any of the herbal dye mixtures for blonde or brown hair can be added to a shampoo mixture; cf. shampoo for Red Hair.

Blonde Hair in Greece and Rome

Blonde hair was much admired in ancient Rome, but the dyes they used tended to make their hair fall out, and so wigs made of the hair of Germans were resorted to. In Greece blonde hair was achieved with a mixture of quince juice and privet; presumably it was made by mixing the juice of quinces with a strong decoction of privet leaves.

Brown Hair Dyes

The Romans used elderberries to give lustre to their dark hair, and to bring out its colour. You can make a pack by mashing elderberries with water – if heated, it is easier to mix them to a smoothish paste. Add a pinch of alum, and mix well in before applying the pack to the hair. On grey hair this has much the same effect as a blue rinse.

Sage

Sage is the best known of country remedies for greying hair, but it needs repeated applications to get any results. Some people consider red sage to be more efficient, while others mix a strong infusion of sage leaves, red or green, with an equal quantity of strong Indian tea. The liquid should be poured through clean, towel-dried hair again and again, and the hair squeezed, but not towelled dry.

Cloves also yield a brown dye, and can be used with sage: bring an ounce of cloves to the boil in ¼ pint of water in an enamel saucepan, simmer covered for half an hour, and then pour the strained decoction over the sage leaves. Allow it to infuse with the lid on until cold. Strain and use.

Walnuts

The use of walnuts to dye the hair brown was recorded by Pliny. Use the skin of the kernel or the leaves of black walnuts. The leaves are easier to deal with; either make a strong infusion, as for sage, or powder the dried leaves, and add enough water to make a thick paste, and proceed as for the chamomile dye. The similarity in appearance between the walnut and the human brain led the old herbalists to use the kernel skin for troubles of the brain, applied as a compress to the crown of the head.

Hands and Feet

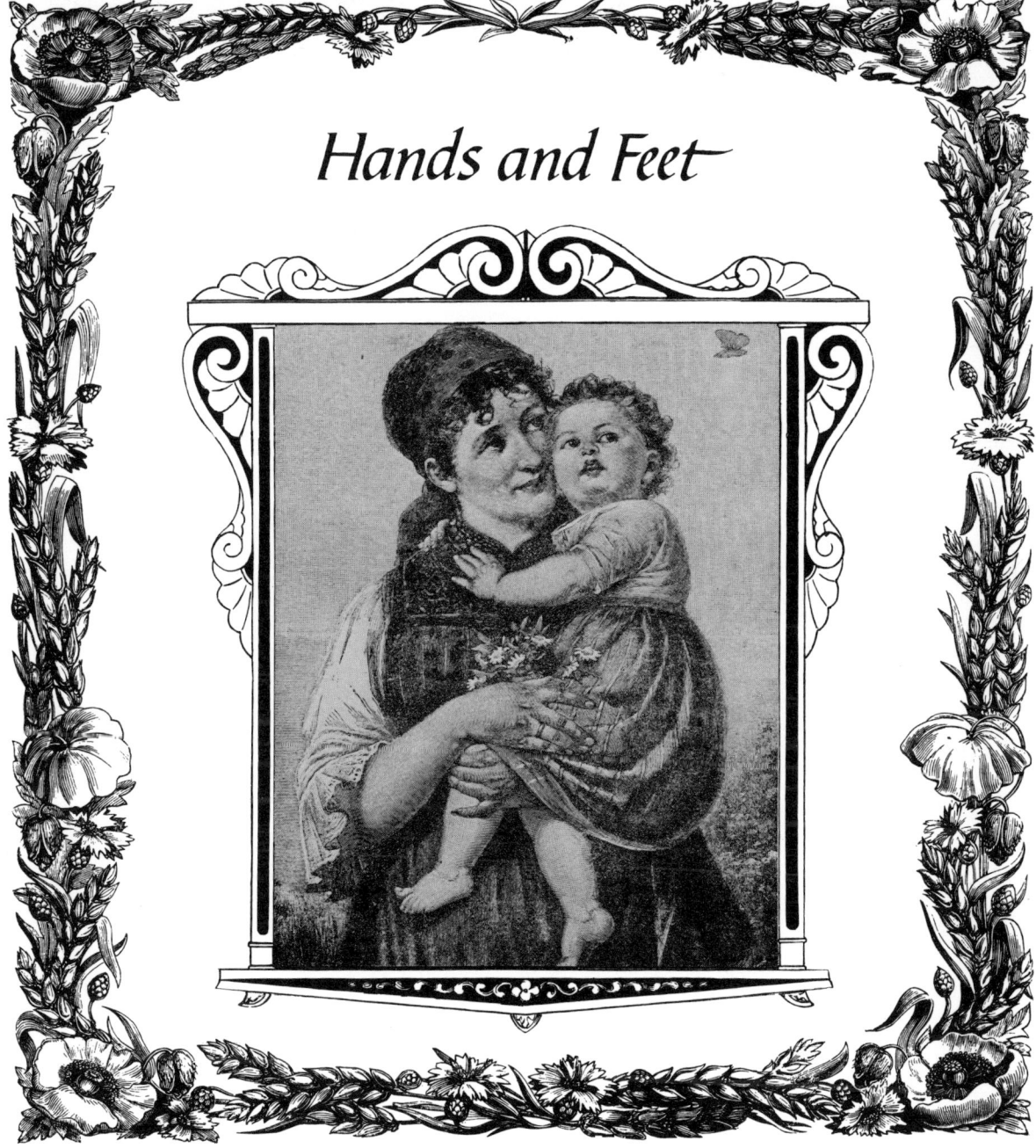

Hands

Finger Nails

'As soon as Dawn with her rose-tinted hands had lit the East.' Homer, *The Odyssey*.

It is said that the expression 'rosy fingered dawn' comes in part from the Egyptian habit of staining the nails pink with henna.

Make a paste with henna and water, and apply it carefully to your finger nails, being careful not to get it on your skin, and allow it to dry completely. Wash off with warm water.

The same thing can be done with powdered alkanet root, which gives a clearer pink with less orange in it.

To colour the Nails

'To give a fine colour to the nails' and make them 'fine and transparent'.

This can be done 'by washing the nails with white horehound water; then rubbing them with Cyprus powder; and afterwards washing them a second time with the water of white horehound.'* *Lady's Toilette*, 1822.

Buffing the Nails

In the 1920s and 1930s it was fashionable to buff the nails to make them shiny and pink. It is certainly much better for them than nail varnish, as it allows them to breathe, and stimulates the circulation.

* White horehound grows on chalk cliffs and downs, and is a silvery plant with white flowers not unlike a white dead nettle.

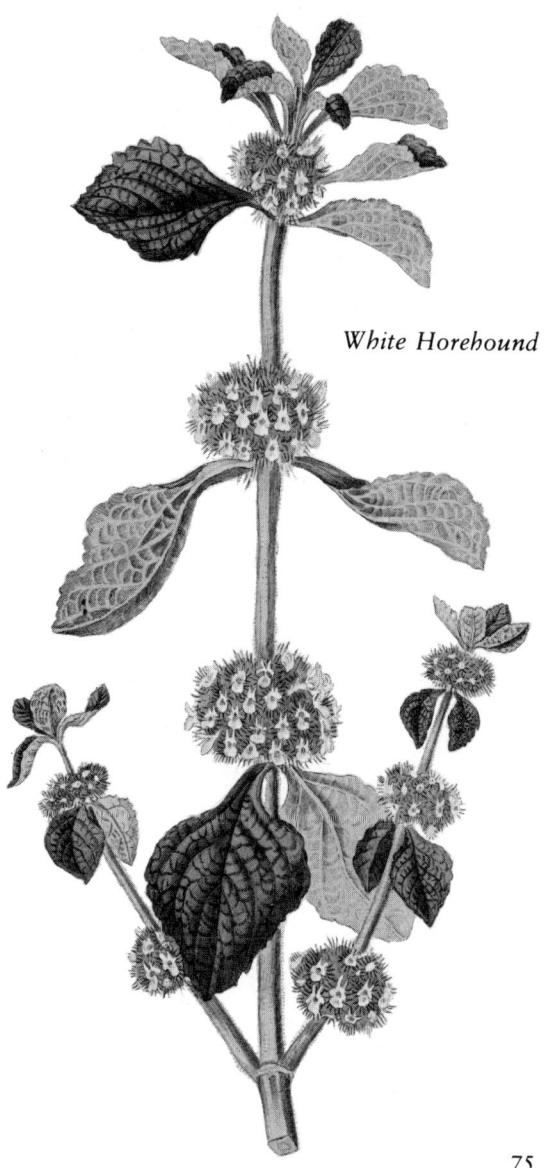

White Horehound

All you need is a piece of chamois leather, a velvet powder puff, and a soft white pencil; polish your nails with the chamois leather wrapped around the powder puff until they shine, and then run the pencil under your nails to whiten them. To make the half-moons look larger the cuticles should be gently pushed back with an orange stick. If you like you can rub a little softened beeswax on your nails before polishing them.

The Right and Wrong Days to cut Nails

A great deal of superstition surrounds the cutting of nails:

'Cut them on Monday, you cut them for health;
Cut them on Tuesday, you cut them for wealth;
Cut them on Wednesday, you cut them for news;
Cut them on Thursday, a new pair of shoes;
Cut them on Friday, you cut them for sorrow;
Cut them on Saturday, you'll see your true love tomorrow;
Cut them on Sunday, and the Devil will be with you all the week'

You should, in fact, never cut them at all or use a metal nail file, as it damages them. Always use an emery board.

To make the Half Moons show on Nails

'... smear the nails of each hand, especially round the half-moon, with warm Vaseline every night. Then wear gloves with the palms slit, but without the tips of the fingers cut off. After a few days have passed, soak your finger-tips in hot milk for ten minutes, and then gently push down the flesh until the half-moons show. It can be done painlessly.'
The Best Way Book

To prevent Redness of the Hands

Mix equal quantities of glycerin and lemon and use it on your hands. Lemon is both cleansing and bleaching.

'Lemon juice and cream will make your hands white. Rub it well in and make it fresh every morning. Lemon juice will whiten the nails if applied with an old match with the end pointed.'
The Best Way Book

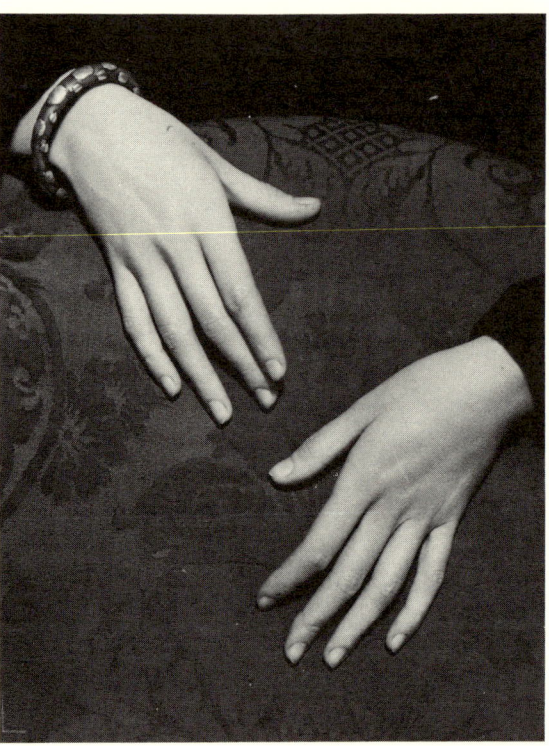

Wearing Gloves at Night

'The reason for wearing an old pair of gloves at night is partly for convenience and partly to improve the hands...' Quite what the author of the *Best Way Book* means is not clear, but most old recipes for making your hands soft and white recommend wearing gloves in bed – whichever cream you choose doesn't get rubbed off on the sheets, and has all night to do its work.

Dry Oatmeal

Baroness Staffe recommends dry oatmeal for the hands. After they have been washed and dried, they should be rubbed with oatmeal. It must be done every night (before putting on your gloves!)

To Make the Hands Soft and White

'Take of Bean and Lupin-Flowers, of each a handful, of Starch, Corn, Rue and Orrice [orris root powder], and Sweet Almonds two Ounces; beat or grind them together, and with the Powder wash your hands often.' Shirley, in *A Chaplet of Herbs*.

Horse Chestnut Paste for the Hands

To clean the hands, and make them white.
 'Peel the chestnuts, dry them, pound them in a covered mortar, and sift the powder through a very fine sieve. To make use of it, put a suitable quantity of this powder into water, which becomes white, saponaceous, and as soft as milk. The frequent use of it is highly salutary, and gives the skin an admirable lustre.' *Lady's Toilette*, 1822.

For Cold and Swollen Hands

'Bath your hands in wine wherein you have boiled nettles, rosemary, thyme, rue, and penny-royal that frequent use of this will keep them from swelling.' Jameson, *Artificial Embellishments*, 1665.

Mallow Hand Cream

3 tablespoons almond oil
1 teaspoon white beeswax
1 tablespoon lanolin
2 tablespoons decoction of mallow roots
6 vitamin E capsules (contents of)

Place the mallow roots in an enamel saucepan and simmer in enough water to cover for 20 minutes with the lid on. Melt the beeswax, the almond oil and the lanolin in a china bowl suspended over a saucepan of boiling water to form a Bain Marie. When they have melted, remove from the heat, and add the strained mallow decoction drop by drop, beating all the time. Add the vitamin E, and continue beating until the cream takes. This happens faster if you place the bowl in another bowl containing cold water. Keep in a covered pot.

Elderflower Ointment for Rough or Chapped Hands

4 oz Vaseline
8 oz fresh elderflowers

Melt the Vaseline in an enamel saucepan, and then put in the elderflowers. Simmer gently for an hour, and then strain the mixture into pots.

Feet

As most treatments for the feet fall within the domain of medicine, this is a very short section of the book, but here are a few tips to keep them looking nice.

To help prevent your Feet from Looking Old

Whenever you have a bath, rub your feet with plenty of oil – cinnamon-scented if you want to follow the Egyptians – as once past the first flush of youth they tend to develop a lot of wrinkles when they are too dry, and show their age.

Pumice Stone

I am sure every one knows about using pumice stone on the hard skin of the feet, but it is important to do it regularly, as once it has got beyond a certain point, and calluses develop, it is too late, and the chiropodist has to be called in.

To prevent the Cuticles from growing over the Nails

The method described above for the finger nails can be followed: rub your toe nails with Vaseline for a few nights, and possibly even wear socks in bed, then soak the nails in hot milk for ten minutes, before pushing back the skin with an orange stick.

Herbal Foot Baths

You can make a strong decoction of any fresh smelling herb, or from a mixture, such as the recipe given for a herb bath for aches and pains (see page 47), and pour it into a bowl. Put your feet in, and cover them with a towel for about ten minutes, or until the water cools. Pansies, flowers and leaves, help to remove hard skin, if the foot bath is repeated often.

To prevent Chilblains

An old recipe against chilblains recommends rubbing the spot where they are likely to strike the following winter, with fresh strawberries in season.

Scent

'... the sense of smell is the sense of the imagination ...'
Rousseau.

Making scent is really quite easy. To make a great one is an art, and how it is done usually remains shrouded in mystery, but many delicious scents, which have been popular for centuries, can be made with very little trouble.

Fashions in scent have changed considerably over the centuries. Although some, like Lavender Water and eau de Cologne, have not gone out of favour, many other good ones, strongly evocative of the times which created them, are no longer made. I have chosen recipes for these lost scents, and for the old favourites, from as many ages and places as possible, as well as for the fresh flowery waters that were once made in every still-room.

Ancient Egypt

When Cleopatra floated down the Nile to meet Mark Anthony, even the winds, according to Shakespeare, were love-sick with the scent of spices. She is supposed to have used 'the worth of 400 denarii of spices but once, to anoint her hands, which was wafted away on the air and lost forever.' Huge quantities of sweet-scented substances were imported: from Babylon came 'oils of cedar, myrrh and cypress', and from the distant land of Punt came frankincense. Sweet rush, or *Calamus aromaticus*, juniper and coriander are mentioned in the earliest records. Although Cleopatra's love of scent became a legend, it is probable that the mysterious Queen Nefertiti, whose name means 'beautiful stranger', was even more strangely and exotically scented than she was.

Kyphi

The most famous of all the ancient perfumes is the sacred Kyphi, which was burnt in the Egyptian temples at sunset as an offering to the setting sun. Plutarch wrote: 'Its aromatic substances lull to sleep, allay anxieties, and brighten the dreams. It is made of things that delight most in the night.' It is, in fact, made of all the sweetest, heaviest spices, with honey and raisins steeped in red wine. It was described by Plutarch, Dioscorides and Galen (who invented the first cold cream), but they vary as to the exact ingredients, which included:

ANDROPOGON SCHOENANTHUS: is lemongrass, which grows in India, the Seychelles and Sri Lanka, and is used in perfumery today.
BDELLIUM: is a form of myrrh.
CALAMUS: also called sweet rush, was until recently one of the most popular of scents. Its roots were used in perfumery from ancient Egypt right through to the pot pourris of the Victorians, and it is mentioned in the Song of Solomon.
CASSIA: also called 'bastard cinnamon', is a relation of the true cinnamon, and is hotter and slightly bitter.
CINNAMON: the bark of a tree native to Sri Lanka, but now cultivated in other tropical countries. The Sabians, inhabitants of the land of Sheba, who traded in cinnamon, claimed that it could only be found in the nest of the Phoenix.
CYPERUS: also called galingale, it is the root of a kind of sedge, rare in Britain, but once used extensively in the making of scents in England.
HENNA: while the leaves produce the well known red dye, a scent called Cyprinum was made from the flowers, whose scent Mohammed described as the best in 'this world and the next'. It is supposed to be the plant used as a hedge in the Hanging Gardens of Babylon.
JUNIPER: its berries have a fresh, clean smell, and

it grows wild on limestone in England and Scotland.

MASTIC: an aromatic gum produced for the most part on the island of Chios, it was dedicated to the moon by the Romans, who burned it on the altar of Diana.

MYRRH: the oldest of perfumes, is an aromatic gum that flows from a shrub native to Arabia and Ethiopia, covering the dry hillsides that slope down to the Red Sea.

PEPPERMINT: the leaves and flowers of the *Mentha piperata*.

SAFFRON: The dried stigmas of the saffron crocus formed the basis of many scents and unguents in the ancient world.

SPIKENARD: or Indian nard, is probably the most legendary of all the ancient aromatics. It was probably used by Mary Magdalene to anoint the feet of Christ, and comes from a species of valerian that grows in the Himalayas. It is sold in Indian bazaars under the name of jatamansi.

A variety of Kyphi can be made, using whichever of these ingredients you can find – some are easier to come by than others! The earliest known recipe says that the calamus, *Andropogon schoenanthus*, mastic, cassia, cinnamon, and peppermint should be dried and powdered, while the juniper, henna and *Cyperus* are to be macerated in wine for a day. Raisins should then be steeped in wine for five days, and a mixture of honey and resin terebinth, or Chio turpentine made. All the ingredients were then to be mixed with the myrrh, and everything mixed together. It also included *Convulvulus scoparius* and *Acacia farnesiana*.

LEFT: *the Hanging Gardens of Babylon. The gardens were cultivated on spacious terraces built over arches*

Other Egyptian Perfumes

The Egyptians made other scents: *Aegyptium* was an oil heavily scented with cinnamon, used to anoint the hands and feet. *Mendesium*, which was made of myrrh and canella, or white cinnamon, steeped in oil of ben, the finest of all the oils. *Metopium* was made of bitter almonds, myrrh, *Calamus*, honey and resin in wine.

White Cinnamon

The Perfumes of Israel

'Who is this that cometh out of the wilderness like pillars of smoke perfumed with myrrh and frankincense with all the powders of the merchant?'

Song of Solomon, 3:6

Sweet Calamus

The Song of Solomon makes frequent reference to aromatic substances and scented flowers: 'Camphire with spikenard; spikenard and saffron; calamus and cinnamon, with all trees of frankincense; myrrh and aloes, with all the chief spices' (4:13–14). All these, with the exception of aloes, are ingredients of the Egyptian Kyphi, and it was from the Egyptians that the Israelites learnt the use of scent and incense. Camphire, another name for henna, was the source of the perfume 'Cyprinum', and is mentioned more than once: 'My beloved is unto me as a cluster of camphire in the vineyards of Engedi' (1:14).

A less well known quotation from the Song of Songs mentions another scent: 'Now also thy breasts shall be as clusters of the vine, and the smell of thy nose like apples' (7:8).

The Holy Anointing Oil

Take 'principal spices, of pure myrrh five hundred shekels, and of sweet cinnamon half so much ... and of sweet calamus two hundred and fifty shekels. And of cassia five hundred shekels, after the shekel of the sanctuary, and of oil olive an hin' (Exodus, 30:23–24). In other words, equal quantities of myrrh and cassia, and half as much of cinnamon and calamus, infused in olive oil.

Babylon, Nineveh and the Garden of Eden

The Garden of Eden is supposed to have been on a flowery plain between the Tigris and the Euphrates, which later fell within the domain of Babylon and Nineveh. The Bible tells us that it was a land of gold and onyx stones, scented with bdellium. When Adam was expelled from this paradise he was allowed, according to Mohammed, to bring with him only three things: an ear of corn, some dates, and a myrtle flower, which shows that the scent of flowers was considered as essential to man as bread. Perhaps because of this legend the nineteenth-century water of myrtle flowers was called:

Eau de Ange

which is made in the following way:

1 lb flowering tops of myrtle
1 pint [Ethyl alcohol] alcohol
8 fl. oz water

Digest for seven days in a stoppered container, add a handful of salt, and distil over half. (Instructions for distilling are to be found on page 90.)

Part of an Arabian caravan

The trade routes from India, Arabia and Syria met in Babylon. Caravans bearing spices from India passed through the land of Sheba in southern Arabia on their way to Babylon, and from there the spices found their way to all the countries of the ancient world. Babylon itself consumed enormous quantities; 1,000 talents of incense were burnt every year on the altar of the golden god Baal in his eight-towered temple – better known to us as the Tower of Babel – and the Babylonians scented their bodies, and burned scented woods in their houses. The hanging gardens, created for his wife Amytes by Nebuchadnezzar, were hedged with henna flowers, and her bower was made of roses and lilies.

Greece

'The finest Extract of Roses in the world was made at Cyrene, while the great Berenice was alive', wrote Apollonius of Herophila, in his long list of

Greek offerings

all the celebrated perfumes of Greece.

Greek perfumery was certainly as sophisticated as Egyptian, and would probably appeal more to modern taste; they used fewer heavy spices and more fresh flowers and sweet-smelling leaves. After the rose, they loved the smell of violets, and mixtures of mint and thyme.

We do not know exactly how they made their scents, but distillation was yet to be developed by the Arabs, and so we can presume that they were 'huiles antiques'.

To make a Huile Antique

This is a very simple process: place the fresh herbs or flowers in a jar with a stopper, filling it up to the top. Pour over them enough oil to cover, and put it in a warm place with the lid on for several days, shaking from time to time. Strain off the oil, pressing it out of the flowers, and put a fresh batch of flowers in the jar. Pour the oil over them, and repeat the process as many times as it takes to give the oil a strong scent.

If 10 per cent wheatgerm oil is used it will help prevent rancidity. The Greeks kept their scents in 'vessels of lead and phials of alabaster', because they believed that extremes of heat and cold caused them to deteriorate quicker. Use the least scented oil you can find: almond, or peach. The scented oils made direct from flowers were lily, mint, thyme, saffron, bergamot and rose, and different places specialised in different scents. Iris was made at Elis and Cyzicus, rose at Naples, Capua and Phaselis, spikenard at Tarsus, marjoram on the island of Cos, frankincense at Pergamus, and 'Extract of Vine Leaves' in Cyprus and Adramyttium.

The garlands with which they adorned their

heads for banquets were made from crocuses, hyacinths, violets, roses and narcissi. Myrtle wreaths were worn, according to Philonides, 'to repress the rising fumes of wine.'

Maceration

I have included this method as it is quite easy, and was used for some of the scented oils made by the ancient Greeks (see 'A Different Scent for Every Part of the Body', below).

The flowers, roots, or fruits (the rind), should be gently simmered at a temperature of 65° Centigrade in oil. Stir frequently to make sure that all the essential oils are released into the oil, bruising the plant well. Strain the oil when you think that all the perfume has been extracted, and repeat the process by pouring the scented oil over a fresh batch of petals or roots. Strain again and bottle. This method is similar to the 'huile antique' process, but it is quicker.

A Different Scent for Every Part of the Body

At one time the leaders of fashion took to using a different scent for each part of the body: the head was scented with apple or rose, the throat and knees with serpolet, which is wild thyme, the hair and eyebrows with marjoram, the arms with wild mint and the neck and lower limbs with essence of ground ivy.

Scents were also made from quince, by macerating the fruit in oil, from gillyflower, or wallflower, made with the flowers, myrtle, from the leaves, and from iris and sweet marjoram, which should be made by macerating the roots in oil, to which has been added a small amount of powdered root of alkanet which will turn it pink. The same should be done for oil of roses.

Rome

The Romans used scent, for the most part, in conjunction with their baths, and so I have included some of their scented oils and unguents in the chapter on the body. They were made in much the same way as the Greek ones. With the exception of lavender, imported from their northern dominions and used liberally in their bath water, they preferred sweeter and spicier scents to the fresh smell of thyme and apples beloved by the Greeks. Amongst their favourite was sweet rush, which can be used as a dry scent – the powdered roots can be used in pot pourris – or the roots can be macerated in oil.

Another was rose oil made from the roses that still grow to this day around the temples of Paestum in the Gulf of Salerno.

Essence of narcissus was much loved in Rome – the heady scent, which the Greek physician Galen

Temples of Paestum

described as the food of the soul, was thought to have narcotic properties – both narcissus and 'narcotic' come from the Greek word for 'stupor'. They had many other scents with strange-sounding names, some dyed blue with myrrh, others black with mendes, such as Medebathrim, Onegalium, Nardinum, and Susinum.

At one time fashion decreed that ladies should be scented by being sprayed with scent from the mouths of their slaves.

In A.D. 565 an edict was passed in Rome forbidding the use of rare spices, except on the altars of the gods. Castus was offered to Saturn, cassia and benzoin to Jove, musk to Juno, aloes to Mars, saffron to the sun, mastic to the moon, cinnamon to Mercury, and ambergris to Venus.

The Scents of the East

Musk and Roses

Rose water was introduced to the medieval world by an Arabian doctor called Avicenna, the 'Prince of Physicians', who distilled it from the petals of the *Rosa centifolia*, or 'gul sad berk', in the tenth century A.D. Its use spread like wildfire; when Saladin conquered Jerusalem in 1187 he had the walls of the great mosque washed with it, and the returning crusaders brought it back to Europe from the Holy Land.

The discovery of true oriental attar of roses came much later. It is said that a Mogul princess, Nour-Djihan Begum, while walking by a canal filled with rose water, noticed small drops of oil glinting in the light – the warmth of the sun had brought the rose otto to the surface.

Attar of roses was certainly made in the Persian city of Shiraz, birthplace of the fourteenth-century poet Hafiz, the 'lover of the rose', after its discovery in 1612. For Hafiz, and the mystics of Shiraz, which was the 'city of perfection', the roses, nightingales, musk and wine that fill his poetry were symbols of God, and the soul's thirst for union with Him. He writes of the Persian Feast of Roses, 'when men are draining flagons to the budding rose', and addressing God he says:

'Roses saw Thy damask cheek
   Dewed with grace; then envy's flame
Scorched them, so in rosewater
   Drowned they then their grief and shame'.
     The Rubaiyat of Hafiz, section 2, verse 1.

To make Rose water

Gather heavily scented roses very early on a fine day, and distil them (see page 90). Pour the rose water into a bottle, put on the lid, and wait for the essential oil, or attar, of roses to float to the top. Remove it with a cotton wool bud, being very careful not to get the cotton wool wet or to leave any oil behind. What remains is pure rose water, which contains all the freshness of the rose without its heavy scent. It has to be removed or the combination of the oil and water will make the rose water go off. Alternatively, do not remove the essential oil and add a chemical preservative or 20 per cent Ethyl alcohol.

To make Attar of Roses

Attar of roses is made by redistilling rose water. It takes enormous quantities of flowers to make even a small amount, which is why it is so expensive, but it is nice to know how it is done. Follow the instructions for making rose water, but do not remove the essential oil that floats to the top. Instead, put a fresh batch of rose petals in the saucepan still, and pour your rose water over them, and distil again in the same way. This time all the scent will come over with the essential oil; the fresh scent which remained behind to make rose water will have become incorporated into the oil, and you will have genuine attar of roses.

To preserve Roses

To have roses all year round, the Arabs put rose buds in an earthenware jar and close the top with clay. The jar is then buried, and left in the earth until the roses are required. When they are dug up they are sprinkled with water, and within a short time their petals open.

An English method of more recent origin is to dip the ends of the stalks of half open roses in sealing wax, wrap the flowers in tissue paper, and place them in an airtight tin. When you want to use them, cut off the part of the stalk covered in sealing wax, and place the flowers in water.

The white rose, according to Arab tradition, was created from the sweat of Mohammed on the 'night of the Mearaj', the red rose from the sweat of the angel Gabriel, who accompanied him, and the yellow rose from the sweat of the beast upon whose back Mohammed rode to Jerusalem, in a dream, before his ascension.

The Koran says that the floor of paradise is made of wheat flour mixed with musk and saffron, and the houris there are made of pure musk. After the rose, musk was probably the Arabs' favourite scent, and it was mixed into the mortar of the great mosque of Zobaide at Tauris, so that when the sun shone on it the walls gave off its scent.

The use of perfume was smiled upon by Allah; it is, says Ib'n Arabi, the great thirteenth-century mystic, one of the three things of this world which give pleasure to God. The other two are wine and women.

Making Scent and Eau de Toilette using Essential Oils and Pure Alcohol

This method is very easy and satisfactory, and is how it is done professionally. You will need the following things:

ETHYL ALCOHOL, which is also known as ETHANOL. It doesn't sound very romantic, but it has been used under other, more old-fashioned names, since the Middle Ages. It is nearly 100 per cent proof – vodka is only 60 or 70 out of 175 – and pure alcohol is needed to dissolve all the elements in an essential oil that go to make up its scent, and to release them on the air. It isn't available neat over the counter, but you can obtain it, with half a per cent of perfume added to it, by mail order from The Cotswold Perfumery Ltd, Bourton-on-the-Water, Gloucestershire. It isn't expensive.

ESSENTIAL OILS which are available from various herbalists and chemists (see list of stockists). There is no easy way of knowing whether they are genuine or synthetic; rose and jasmine, for instance, are fabulously expensive to buy, so these will probably be artificial, while lavender, bergamot, orange, lemon, etc. are cheaper to produce, and so more likely to be the real thing. Even then no hard and fast rules can be made, because it is possible in many cases to produce an 'essential oil' synthetically which does not differ chemically in any way from the oil given by the plant it imitates. However, with the cheaper oils it is safer to stick to the fresher smelling scents; imitations of sweet flowers can be very cloying, while most cheap copies of musk and ambergris are to be avoided. For this reason I have not included any of the heavy scents of Tudor and Stuart times, as they usually contain musk, civet, and ambergris.

The addition of a little oil of clary sage is said to remove the synthetic smell of artificially produced oils.

DARK GLASS BOTTLES – Light destroys perfume, as does a constant change in temperature, so keep your scents in dark bottles in a cool place.

GLASS DROPPERS – You will need as many glass droppers as essential oils – they should be very fine and narrow, giving a small drop, so that you can achieve precision. These can be cleaned by immersing them in a jug of warm water with a little washing up liquid. Rinse, and leave to dry in a warm place. Breakages can be avoided by putting a Kleenex in the bottom of the jug. When they are dry, rinse them out with a little Ethyl alcohol.

These droppers are also available from The Cotswold Perfumery, Bourton-on-the-Water, Glos.

Distillation

I have included recipes for two different types of eau de toilette or floral water. The first type, which is the simplest and cheapest, is made of nothing but flowers, or leaves, and water with the addition of a little alcohol to preserve it. The second, which is a bit more complicated, is described on page 91.

Floral Waters

You will need the following equipment: a large enamel saucepan with a rounded lid, and without a plastic handle, a smaller Perspex bowl, something round to hold the bowl off the floor of the saucepan, and some smooth pebbles for the bottom of the saucepan.

It is best to use flowers or leaves that have a very strong scent. Jasmine, sweet pea, mignonette and violets, are too delicate, and cannot be distilled. Another method is usually used for these, called enfleurage (see page 91).

It is quite easy once you get the hang of it. It will probably help if you place a layer of small, rounded stones on the bottom of the saucepan first to prevent it burning, or add some salt. Place the flowers or leaves, from which all stalks and bits have been removed, around the smaller bowl on the bottom of the pan. Cover the flowers with water – you want enough water to stop the flowers burning, but not so much as to make the final product too weakly scented. Put the lid of the saucepan on upside down, and put the saucepan on the heat. As the water starts to boil, fill the upturned lid with ice. The hot steam will rise, and as it meets the cold lid it will condense, run down, and fall into the small bowl below. Allow it to boil, but not too violently, for five or ten minutes, by which time most of the essential oil will have distilled over with some of the water into the small bowl. Don't go on for too long, or the distillate, as it is called, will get weaker and weaker. Lavender may take up to twenty minutes, but other flowers and leaves will take a much shorter time. You can experiment by removing what you have got after five minutes, then replacing the bowl for a second batch, and seeing if it is still as strong. Add 20 per cent of Ethyl alcohol or a chemical preservative, and put the lid on immediately to prevent evaporation.

To make Concentrated Flower Waters

If you want to make a more strongly scented water, when you have finished the process described above add the same amount (weight) of Ethyl alcohol to the distilled flower water as you used flowers in the first place: i.e. if you used 6 oz of flowers, add 6 oz of alcohol. Distil this mixture, and when less than half has come over into the small bowl, it will contain all the scent of the flowers.

Another Method

Some of the recipes included follow a slightly different procedure. The flowers, leaves, or spices are macerated for a varying number of days in a mixture of, say, rose water and Ethyl alcohol, before they are distilled in the same way as in the original method.

Enfleurage

Enfleurage is used mostly for jasmine, tuberose, and orange blossom. Sheets of glass supported by wooden frames are smeared with lard or oil and stacked one on top of another. The petals of the flowers are spread quite thickly on the fat, and sandwiched between the layers. Fresh flowers replace the old ones every day or so. Eventually the scent is strong enough and you have made a pommade.

The Middle Ages

Eau de Chypre

When Richard Cœur de Lion became 'King of Cyprus' during the Crusades, eau de Chypre, one of the most famous of the old scents, was introduced into Europe. 'During the national career of Egypt, Persia, Greece and Rome, the island of Cyprus was the resort of the élite, learned, and refined,' says Piesse in his *Art of Perfumery*. Whether or not eau de Chypre really came from Cyprus no one really knows, but in medieval Europe it became a symbol of the far-off, voluptuous life of the harems, which the returning crusaders described.

In the sixteenth century it was used as a dry perfume containing calamus, coriander, benzoin, calaminth and storax mixed together, but by the eighteenth century it was made of quite different things.

Here is a recipe:

Add equal quantities of essential oil of roses and of musk, and half the amount of essential oils of vanilla, ambergris, tonquin bean, and orris root, to some Ethyl alcohol. You can make it as strong or weak as you like, depending on whether you want a proper scent, or just an eau de toilette.

Lavender Water

Saint Hildegarde, a Benedictine abbess of the twelfth century, who is famous for her mystical visions, is said to have invented Lavender Water; it was certainly being made in England, France and Germany in the early Middle Ages. The best lavender in the world is supposed to grow in England. Although Mitcham in Surrey, where it was grown for centuries, no longer produces it, it still grows in Kent, Norfolk and Suffolk, where English oil of lavender is now produced. French oil of lavender, which I prefer, is not considered to be of nearly such high quality.

There are several ways of making it. You can make a simple distillation with water, which is suitable for use on the face (see page 19), but if you want to use it as a scent, add essential oil of lavender to Ethyl alcohol either on its own, or with small amounts of other flower oils. Jasmine softens it, so does rose, but you can add anything you like. One of the most popular Victorian versions contained lavender and 'Eau de Millefleurs', which was a mixture of almost every sweetly scented flower you can think of. It was originally made by distilling the flowers with Aqua Vitae.

Hungary Water

Hungary Water was named after Queen Elizabeth of Hungary, who, it is said, was given the recipe by a hermit in the late fourteenth century. The hermit received it from an angel. It made Elizabeth

Queen Elizabeth of Hungary

so beautiful that the King of Poland asked for her hand in marriage when she was seventy-two.

The earliest recipe says that it was made by distilling the tips of rosemary flowers, verbena and rose water with alcohol, but you can make it by adding to 2 fluid ounces of Ethyl alcohol the following:

30 drops essential oil of rosemary
12 drops essential oil of lemon
5 drops essential oil of rose
5 drops essential oil of orange flower
4 drops essential oil of lemon balm
1 drops essential oil of peppermint

Many versions of Hungary Water are made with rosemary and sage, so you can add some to this recipe, or substitute it for the lemon or orange flower.

The Perfumes of the Tudors

In the sixteen century the fashion for the heady, overpowering, animal scents of musk, civet and ambergris reached England from Italy. Often mixed with damask roses, and with every conceivable spice, they formed the basis of nearly all the perfumes of the time. Henry VIII's favourite scent was made of ambergris and roses with a little sugar and musk, and Elizabeth I, whose love of these strong scents helped establish the fashion in England, loved the mixture of musk and roses. She wore scented shoes, a cloak of 'peau d'Espagne', which was leather saturated in civet or musk, and was the first in England to carry a pomander. Pomanders were not as we know them now, an orange stuck with cloves – they were mixtures of aromatic gums such as benzoin and storax, mixed with the inevitable civet, musk and ambergris, rolled up into a ball.

Necklaces were made of the same mixture rolled into small balls and strung together, and embroidered leather gloves were elaborately scented with a perfume called frangipani, made from a mixture of every known spice, their weight again in orris powder, and a grain of musk and civet.

Civet

The Eighteenth Century

Madame de Pompadour and Marie Antoinette

Madame de Pompadour introduce into this pungent atmosphere the scent of flowers. She loved hyacinths most of all, and surrounded herself with them, but she used many other flowery scents. Marie Antoinette, who reintroduced the fashion for sweet-smelling baths, followed suit, and wore scents made of violets and roses. It is thanks to her that

Advertisement for perfume, from La Mode, *1895*

the heavy perfumes of the Renaissance gave way to the fresh, flowery scents we like today.

As musk, civet and ambergris are all animal products, and are anyway almost unobtainable, and very expensive, I have not included the recipes that use them. Synthetic imitations are not at all good, and civet itself has one of the nastiest smells you can find.

Eau de Cologne

The original eau de Cologne was invented by an Italian called John Maria Farina at the beginning of the eighteenth century. It enjoyed little success under its original name of 'Kölnisches Wasser', but it became popular with the French soldiers stationed in Cologne, where it was made, who referred to it as 'eau admirable', and 'eau de Cologne'. Only later, with the addition of a little rosemary, did it officially change its name and really catch on. It is hard to imagine what a revolution it caused; Lavender Water and Hungary Water had, until then, been the only fresh-smelling scents available, and the fashion for heavy spices and for musk and civet had lasted for three hundred years. Napoleon is said to have used sixty bottles in a month, and to have insisted that the Empress Josephine, who loved the scent of musk, should wear it in his presence.

Farina's Recipe

To make:

   1 gallon alcohol (pure) (use Ethyl alcohol)
   9 drachms oil of bergamot
   9 drachms oil of Portugal (oil of orange peel)
  10 drachms oil of neroli
  10 drachms oil of petigrain
   8 drachms oil of lemon
   8 drachms oil of lavender
   8 drachms oil of rosemary

These quantities are rather large, but it shows the proportions needed. You don't have to have all the ingredients – there are countless variants of eau de Cologne, which basically consists of a mixture of 'citrus' scents with lavender or rosemary. Later colognes add sweeter, floral notes to the original recipe, such as wallflower, jasmine and rose.

The Nineteenth Century

'... After the indifference and incuriosity of the First Empire, which used eau-de-Cologne and rosemary to excess, perfumery followed Victor Hugo and Gautier and went for inspiration to the lands of the sun ...', wrote Huysmans in *A Rebours* in 1884, looking back on the scents of the nineteenth century.

The Victorian era saw the invention of strange new scents based on 'the cult of things Chinese and Japanese'. The perfumers spent their time, Huysmans continues, 'mingling lavender and clove to produce the perfume of the Rondeletia, marrying patchouli and camphor to obtain the singular aroma of China ink, combining citron, clove, and neroli to arrive at the odour of the Japanese Hovenia.'

Rondeletia

One of the most famous scents of the nineteenth century, it is made as follows:

Add to 2 fluid ounces of Ethyl alcohol:

25 drops essential oil of lavender
10 drops essential oil of cloves
10 drops essential oil of bergamot
 2 drops essential oil of vanilla
 2 drops essential oil of rose
 4 drops essential oil of clary sage

Queen Victoria in Grasse, visiting a distillery in a French perfume factory

THE MOST FASHIONABLE PERFUMES

Distilled from Fresh Flowers

BY

J. GIRAUD FILS,
GRASSE,
VENICE, and OLYMPIA.

Violettes de Grasse, 5/-, 2/6.
Violettes de Nice, 6/-, 4/6, 3/-.
Vanda, 4/6, 2/6.
Australian Bouquet, 3/6, 2/6.
Violettes d'Italie, 5/-, 3/6, 2/6.
White Lilac, 3/6, 2/6.
Lys du Japon, 3/6, 2/6.
Bouquet Fleurs de Grasse, 6/-, 4/6, 3/-.

H.M. Queen Victoria, when in Grasse, pronounced the Perfumes of M. Giraud to be "Exquisite."

Sachets of Artistic Design and Delicious Fragrance, from 6d. each.

Of all leading Chemists and Perfumers, or the London Agents.

Hovenia

'... hovenia that makes men mad ...' Oscar Wilde.

Add to 2 fluid ounces of Ethyl alcohol the following:

24 drops essential oil of lemon
2 drops essential oil of neroli
4 drops essential oil of cloves
8 drops essential oil of rose

Tea Rose

Add to 2 fluid ounces of Ethyl alcohol the following:

16 drops essential oil of rose
8 drops essential oil of geranium
4 drops essential oil of sandalwood
2 drops essential oil of neroli
2 drops essential oil of orris

Water of Pinks

From Baroness Staffe's *Lady's Toilette* 1892.

8 oz petals of pinks
1 pint alcohol

'Infuse the petals in the alcohol for ten days, then strain through paper, and add 4 ounces of tincture of benzoin.' If you can't find simple tincture of benzoin, dilute some essential oil of benzoin in Ethyl alcohol. (Ethyl alcohol must be used to infuse the pinks.)

Other Floral Waters

Any strongly scented leaf will produce a delicious-smelling water if distilled by the water method described on page 90. For instance, rose geranium, rosemary, thyme, bay, etc.

Pot Pourri and Sachets for Clothes

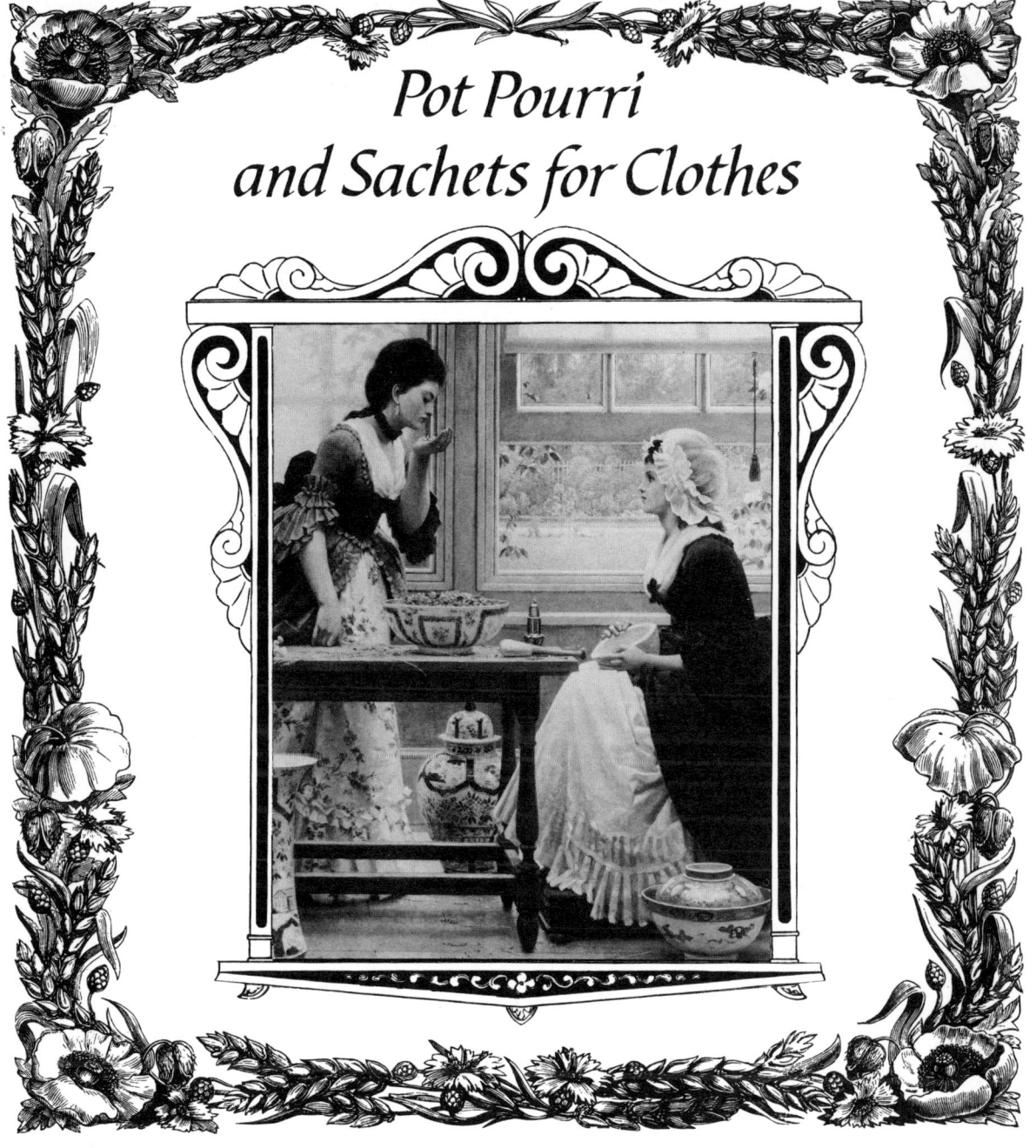

Gathering Flowers, Drying and Storing

Young flowers and leaves should be gathered in the morning after the dew has dried, and before the sun is hot. It is better to wait until there have been a few dry days, as if the flowers are at all wet, they may turn mouldy. Be careful not to bruise them, and lay them out on sheets of paper in a warm, dry place away from the light. An airing cupboard is ideal. The flowers should be scattered thinly on the paper, and turned from time to time. When they are dry, place them in large, sealed paper bags – many people recommend storing them in sealed jars, but they do better if they have a little air. Flowers which have petals that contain a lot of moisture should be dried in white sand, as should flower buds, or anything similar which it is difficult for the air to reach and dry out. Fill the bottom of a tin with white sand, place the flowers on it so they don't touch each other, and sprinkle a fine layer of sand over the top, and put it in a very warm place. Make sure the sand is dry before using it.

To make Pot Pourri

When you have chosen the mixture of scented flowers, leaves and fixatives that you want, select some brightly coloured flowers to give the whole thing colour. Cornflowers, hollyhocks, pansies, wallflowers, marigolds, lavender, borage, broom and pinks all keep their colour well when dried. Green mixtures without any flowers also look fresh and pretty.

Once your flowers and leaves are dry, fill a large jar with them, and add the bay salt and any other fixative you are using (see below). Stir thoroughly with a wooden spoon, and pour out the mixture into open bowls.

Broom

Fixatives

You can make pot-pourri from almost any scented flower, leaf or spice, but you will need fixatives to make them last. Here are some of the things you can use:

dried orange peel
dried tangerine peel
dried lemon peel
powdered orris root – this is one of the best, with a delicate, violet scent which can be added to any mixture.
benzoin – either powdered, or a few drops of the essential oil – it has a very soft, pleasant smell. Add to the other fixatives before mixing them in with the flowers.
cinnamon – use broken-up sticks.
nutmeg – if you grind it yourself it will have a stronger, fresher scent.
cloves
mace – use all the spices sparingly unless you want a very spicy mixture.
vanilla pods
tonquin beans – these are really delicious, smelling of new-mown hay.
calamus – one of the best – use the powdered root.
allspice berries

You can add a few drops of essential oil as a fixative also – for instance, sandalwood oil, clary sage oil, myrrh, bergamot.

Bay Salt – a Fixative

There seems to be some confusion as to what bay salt really is. Many people use ordinary coarse sea salt on its own, but here is another version. Grind

up a quantity of fresh bay leaves in a coffee grinder or mixer, and add an equal quantity of coarse salt. It smells wonderful, and is one of the best ways of releasing the scent from the bay leaves, which are one of the most suitable ingredients for pot pourris.

A Spicy Carnation Mixture

4 oz dried pinks
2 oz dried carnations
2 oz dried, crushed bay leaves
1 oz cloves
2 oz orris powder
2 oz bay salt (made with powdered bay leaves)
¼ oz mace
2 oz dried wallflowers
2 oz dried sweet williams
2 oz red rose petals

A Very Pretty Mixture

6 oz dried red rose petals
4 oz dried leaves of lemon balm (*Melissa*)
2 oz dried jasmine flowers
1 oz pansies
1 oz pinks
2 oz dried mint
2 oz dried cornflowers
1 oz dried marigold petals
2 oz bay salt (made with powdered bay leaves)
2 oz powdered orris root
1 oz powdered benzoin, or 10 drops of essential oil of benzoin
   Note: these quantities are meant only as a guide to proportions.

Green Pot Pourri

4 oz scented geranium leaves
2 oz leaves of lemon balm
2 oz leaves of lemon verbena
2 oz bay leaves
2 oz mint leaves (as many varieties as possible)
1 oz rosemary
1 oz thyme
1 oz buds of balsam poplar (must be gathered in spring, when they first appear, as they lose their scent as soon as they open)
4 oz cistus leaves
2 oz bay salt
2 oz powdered orris root
2 oz dried lemon peel (without pith)
2 oz powdered benzoin, or 10 drops of essential oil of benzoin
10 drops of essential oil of geranium

Rose Pot Pourri

4 oz Damask rose petals (or other strongly scented rose)
2 oz of any striped rose (red and white York and Lancaster; red and pink *Rosa mundi*; the flower of the alchemists; Tricolor de Flandre, or the dark and pale pink dappled rose La Plus Belle des Ponctuées)
1 oz scented white rose petals, or any colour you prefer
1 oz cinnamon – broken-up sticks
1 oz nutmeg
1 oz pinks
1 oz pansies, or mauve violas
1 oz borage flowers
2 oz bay salt
2 oz powdered orris root
10 drops essential oil of benzoin

It is not necessary to keep to the better known mixtures for pot pourris and sachets. Here are

Gathering the new-mown hay

2 oz melilot flowers
2 oz sweet vernal grass
1 oz tonquin beans
1 oz chamomile flowers

All these plants, except vanilla and chamomile, contain coumarin, which gives new-mown hay its scent. Most of them develop their perfume only when dry, so don't be discouraged if they don't smell when you pick them.

Sweet woodruff, or *Galium odoratum*, is a delicate woodland plant with white flowers, growing to about one foot. It is common on calcareous soil, and has stars of pointed leaves at intervals up the stalk. It flowers between May and June.

Melilot: the name means 'honey lotus'.

Sweet vernal grass, or *Anthoxanthum odoratum* gives new-mown hay its scent, as it contains coumarin.

Tonquin beans, used by the Creoles to keep off moths and insects, have a strong scent of new-mown grass. They are a native of Brazil, Guiana, and that part of Nicaragua known as the Mosquito Coast. They are obtainable from some herbalists (see list of stockists), and are really worth getting. The Creoles scatter them loose amongst their clothes to protect them.

You can leave out the chamomile and vanilla if you want a purer version.

some which will help protect clothes from moths and insects, or give them, or your room, an unusual scent.

'New-Mown Hay'

3 chopped up vanilla pods
2 oz sweet woodruff

For the Scent of Orange Groves

3 oz orange blossom
3 oz leaves of orange and lemon tree
1 oz dried orange peel
1 oz dried lemon peel
½ oz calamus root

If you cannot find orange or lemon leaves, add a

few drops of oil of petitgrain, which is made from the leaves of the bitter orange tree. This mixture, especially without the leaves, is better for a sachet (see page 104), because of the large quantities of powdered ingredients.

Here is a more complicated version of the same thing, using the ingredients that go to make up eau de Cologne:

Eau de Cologne Pot Pourri

1 oz eau de Cologne mint
1 oz orange and lemon leaves
1 oz orange blossoms
½ oz dried orange peel
½ oz dried lemon peel
½ oz lavender
½ oz rosemary
½ oz jasmine flowers
½ oz rose petals
5 drops essential oil of bergamot

If you can't find the orange and lemon leaves, substitute 5 drops of oil of petigrain.

A Pot Pourri against the Plague

This mixture, given by Master Alexis the Piedmontese, in his sixteenth-century book of secrets, was to be 'stamped together', and 'set upon the coales' to burn, and so fumigate the room. All the ingredients were powerful against infection and disease. It was made of 'Mastich, Chypre, Incense, Mace, Wormwood, Myrrh, Aloes-wood, Musk, Ambergris, Nutmegs, Myrtle, Bay, Rosemary, Sage, Roses, Elder, Cloves, Juniper, Rue, and Pitch'. A mixture of some of these might be good for a sick room.

Juniper

Another Germ Killer

Modern medicine has found that many herbs, and their aromatic oils, do kill germs. Here is a pot pourri based on them:

6 sticks cinnamon (broken up)
1 oz cloves
½ oz juniper berries
¼ oz lemon peel
1 oz verbena leaves
½ oz thyme
½ oz lavender
10 drops essential oil of tuberose
5 drops essential oil of sandalwood

Sachets and other Dry Scents

To make Sachets for Clothes

Although the same mixtures can be used for both, sachets differ from pot pourri in several ways. The ingredients must be powdered, and bay salt, for instance, omitted. As well as the sweet-smelling things that go into a pot pourri, they include plants that discourage insects from eating your clothes. Grind up the dried ingredients in a coffee mill, and sew them into small bags made of a finely woven material that will not allow the powders to leak out.

Elizabeth I's 'Dry Perfume'

Take 'Of Compound water 8 spoonfuls, the weight of two pence in fine powdered sugar, and boil it on hot embers softly, and half an ounce of sweet marjoram, dried in the sun, and the weight of two pence of the powder of benjamin. When dried this powder is very sweet.'

Compound water was a mixture of rose water and damask water; benjamin is benzoin.

'Damask Powder'

Presumably the 'damask water' that went to make 'Compound water' must have been related to this dry sachet scent so much loved by the Elizabethans. 'Take petals from the Damask rose and mix with Musk, Storax, Labdanum, Gum-benzoin, Gallingal, and Calamus, and you will have a fine odour.' 1563. Labdanum is the resin of the *Cistus* plant, common in the Mediterranean; Gallingal is the root of a rare sedge, with a very sweet scent.

The 'Sachet Powder' of Queen Isabella of Spain

'Take rose leaves, orris-root, calamus, storax, benzoin, girofle flowers (wallflowers), and coriander, and rub them to a powder, then mix them with great care.'

'A Violette Powder for the Perfuming of Linen used by the King Henry of France'

It is made of 'Orris root, rose leaves, santal wood, cypres, benjamen, marjoleine, storax, calamus, giroffle, ambergris, coriander and lavender.' The ingredients are to be dried, powdered and mixed, then put into sachets. Cypres – the fresh twigs and cones of the cypress tree; benjamen – benzoin; marjoleine – marjoram; giroffle – wallflower.

Indian Shawls

The Indian cashmere shawls, so coveted by the Victorians, were scented with patchouli. It was a long time before English manufacturers discovered what gave them their haunting scent, and so it was always easy to recognise the genuine, exotic article.

Queen Isabella of Spain

Dried patchouli leaves had been placed amongst the folds to protect them from moths.

Once the secret had been discovered dried, ground patchouli leaves were used extensively to make sachets to protect wool and linen.

'White Rose' Sachet

Mix three parts powdered rose petals with one part powdered patchouli leaves, and place in a satin envelope, muslin bag, or other container.

The scent of patchouli, which Piesse compared to the smell of 'old coats', when mixed with red rose petals creates the scent of white roses. If you cannot find dried patchouli leaves, sprinkle a few drops of patchouli oil over the powdered petals, and mix in well.

'Satan smells of Sulphur, and I smell of Orris Root'

So says a 'great lady', quoted by Baroness Staffe in the *Lady's Dressing Room* in 1892. Victorian women believed that a lady should choose one scent and never be unfaithful to it, using it to perfume 'all her belongings, her books, her note-paper, her boudoir, the cushions of her carriage ...', which would evoke memories of her. Some women, Baroness Staffe continues, use only the fresh flowers and herbs that are in season, placing them in their cupboards, in the pockets of their clothes, and in muslin sachets, where they are allowed to fade and dry, imparting their delicate scent to all their clothes. Violets, roses and mignonette were favourites.

Flower Sachets for the Winter

These same women made up muslin bags from 'melilot, meadowsweet, and aspernla [asperula, another name for sweet woodruff], dried in the shade' to be used in the winter, so that 'When they pass you by, they remind you of meadows full of flowers.'

Scented Cupboards

Cupboards lined with cedarwood or rosewood, which now, unfortunately, are hard to come by, not only scented the clothes kept in them, but protected them from moths. Bags filled with wood shavings of these scented trees will do the same. Another Victorian custom was to line drawers and shelves with thin satin quilting padded with scented cotton wool, so that everything lay 'upon beds of perfumed satin'.

The favourite scent was sewn into the hems of dresses, and into the folds of sleeves.

Scented Shells

Perfumed shells were used in the nineteenth century to scent jewellery boxes, sewing baskets, and such like. In those days they used 'Venetian shells', found on the shores of the Adriatic, but any spiralled shell will do. Soak them in a mixture of essential oils. The classic mixture was bergamot, with half as much sandalwood, even less lavender and rosewood, and a trace of musk and civet.

To Scent Writing Paper

Place the sheets of paper between two pieces of blotting paper which have been soaked in essential oils, and then dried. If you try to scent it directly, it will spoil the paper. In medieval Japan, we are told by Shikibu Murasaki, the endless love letters which were exchanged by people whom etiquette hardly allowed to meet, consisted of one verse of poetry on coloured and scented writing paper. Each scent expressed a different shade of feeling, which had been left unsaid by the poetry.

Vetivert Blinds

In Calcutta, awnings, blinds and sunshades were made out of Vetivert, or Kus-Kus, which, when sprinkled with water in the hot weather, gave out a delicious scent. Vetivert was also used to protect Indian muslin from moths and insects, and the

Sumptuous setting for ladies of Cabul

material arrived in England perfumed with the delicate scent so popular during the Indian Raj.

Mousseline des Indes – Indian muslin – was one of the great scents of the nineteenth century. Here is Piesse's recipe for a Mousseline Sachet.

1 lb Vitivert, in powder (root)
½ lb Santal-wood ⎫ of each
     Orris   ⎭
¼ lb Black-currant leaves (cassis)
¼ lb Benzoin, in powder
5 drops Otto of thyme
½ drachm Otto of roses

All the ingredients should be ground in a mill, or coffee grinder, and then put in silk or muslin bags, or pretty envelopes.

Scented Cushions

Cushions and pillows can be stuffed with any number of aromatic herbs and flowers. In the eighteenth century carriage cushions were filled with a mixture called 'herbes de Montpellier'. Montpellier was the centre of the French perfumery business in those days. Charles VI of France also had satin cushions filled with lavender.

'A Bag to smell unto for Melancholy, or to cause one to sleep'

'Take drie Rose leaves, keep them close in a glasse which will keep them sweet, then take powder of Mints, powder of Cloves in a grosse powder, and put the same to the Rose leaves, then put all these together in a bag, and take that to bed with you, and it will cause you to sleep, and it is good to smell unto at other times.'

Ram's Little Dodoen, 1606

A flower seller

A Pillow filled with Sleep-Inducing Herbs

Take equal quantities of dried hops and dried lime blossoms. Wrap them in a double thickness of cotton or linen – a piece of old sheeting will do – and then place them inside a pillow case.

Rosemary, lavender, jasmine and chamomile are also said to induce sleep, so try a mixture of any of these. Lemon verbena is supposed to have an aphrodisiac scent.

A Citronella-Scented Candle to keep off Insects and Mosquitoes

Melt two candles in an enamel saucepan, and remove the wicks. Pour the wax into a small bowl that can take heat, and add 20 or 30 drops of essential oil of citronella. As the wax begins to solidify insert a wick, and cut it down to the right size.

Any other scent can be used instead of the citronella, but it will not deter mosquitoes.

Scenting the Room

'The perfuming-pan, which was kindled in the palaces of Babylonia, Susa, and Venice, still smokes in the seraglios of Teheran, and on the shores of the Bosphorus,' Septimus Piesse.

Edward VI's Rose Scent for the Room

' ... take 12 spoonfulls of bright red rose-water, the weight of sixpence in fine powder of sugar, and boyl it on hot Embers and coals softly, and the house will smell as though it were full of Roses; but you must burn sweet Cypress wood before, to take away the gross ayre.'
From *The Queen's Closet Opened*, by W.M. Cook to Queen Henrietta Maria, 1665.

The air is not quite as gross nowadays as it was in Tudor times, so the last part can be omitted.

Juniper Branches

In the seventeenth century there was a great demand for juniper wood: 'The smoke of Juniper is in great request with us to sweeten our chambers,' wrote Burton in the *Anatomy of Melancholy*; it is certainly one of the nicest ways of scenting any room. Juniper is a shrub with pointed leaves which is common on limestone, growing to about ten feet, mostly in Scotland and the Lake District. If you can find it growing by the wayside, take home a few dead branches, or carefully cut one or two living ones so that the tree is not damaged, and let them dry out thoroughly before using them. When you want to use it, stick the end in the fire until it lights, then blow it out, and wave the smoking branch around the room.

Strewing the Floor

Although the habit of strewing the floor with sweet-smelling plants died out long ago, to this day churches in Greece are scattered with bay leaves which give off a sweet scent as they are walked upon, and in some parts of Spain lavender is still used for the same purpose.

In medieval and Tudor England houses and churches were scented in this way. Hay was used, for the smell of coumarin in the sweet vernal grass, and yellow flag irises. The great herbalist, Gerard, recommended water mint and meadowsweet. Churches were strewn with a carpet of sweet-smelling flowers.

During the seventeenth century sweet sedge, or *Calamus aromaticus*, which was a native of the Near East, escaped from the botanical gardens and naturalised itself in England. From then on its strong, orangey scent filled the houses of all those who could find it or afford it. Although it is not a very practical way of making a room smell sweet, particularly with fitted carpets, the scent must have been far better and fresher than any man-made perfume.

Magic, Charms and Love Potions

In the quest for charms and love potions, and for plants of magical power, we enter a timeless, pagan world. Through many centuries of Christianity the old gods, deposed and exiled to the woods and fields, continued to exert their power. Nature was alive with their half-forgotten presence, and with the spirits who personified the plants, trees and stones. Some plants had more 'mana', or power, than others to heal, to bewitch, to make beautiful or to grant second sight, and these had to be treated with respect by those who gathered them if they were not to lose their power. Charms and incantations were recited over them when they were picked to pacify their guardian spirits and to ensure their co-operation, or to keep the forces of evil at bay.

The Right Time to gather Magical Herbs

The full moon was usually considered to be the best moment to go out and gather herbs for spells and potions. The moon ruled over the growth and decay of nature, and so the properties of plants were at their height when the moon was full. The ancient association between night, the moon, and witchcraft also played a part; Hecate, goddess of the moon and of witches, imbued the herbs with her occult powers and increased their magical potency. Dawn was the other time to gather plants, and fasting beforehand was often recommended. At dawn the magical herbs were still covered in dew, and dew, which appeared during a cloudless night as though by magic, was thought to possess great powers. The dew of May Day morning was the best, but any would do, and it was used in cosmetics and in magic.

Druids gathering mistletoe for a ceremony

Ancient Druids

Magical Plants

The Herbs of the Druids

The sacred plants of the Druids were the oak, the mistletoe, and vervain. The oak is the tree of the midsummer solstice, the moment when the sun has reached its zenith and is about to decline. For the Druids, who celebrated the dying and returning year, the oak symbolised the forces of life at their most powerful, and their name is supposed by some to mean 'those who have knowledge of the Oak', or 'those with deep knowledge'.

Mistletoe, which grows on the oak, protected men from evil, and was allegedly used as a cure for sterility, as an antidote for poison and as a miracle cure. The Druids cut the mistletoe from the oak with golden knives early in the year, and then only when they received a vision telling them to do so. In later ages it was used as a cure for epilepsy, delirium, and St Vitus's dance, which was a common disease in the Middle Ages. In large doses, however, it can cause convulsions, and it is a narcotic. It grows most often on apple trees, especially in Herefordshire, but also upon the 'Oak, Ash and Thorn'. Although the mistletoe from an oak is supposed to be the most powerful, it is not often found, except, I am told, in America. It is very unlucky, they say, if it falls to the ground when it is cut.

Vervain was used by the Druids for magic and healing, and the Druidesses are supposed to have worn wreaths of it. They gathered it 'under the Dog Star' (the first week or ten days of July are called the Dog Days because the Romans believed that Sirius, the Dog Star, was then at its height and added its heat to that of the Sun), and used it in their holy water. It was known in later days as the 'Enchanter's herb', and a room sprinkled with vervain water was said to make the heart glad and dispel gloom.

Although Vervain's Latin name is *Verbena*, it must not be confused with lemon verbena, which was introduced into England in the eighteenth century. The original *Verbena*, which means 'altar-plant', was much used in sacrifices in Rome, as well as by the Druids. It was long believed to have aphrodisiac qualities, and is an ingredient of many love potions.

Other Magical Plants of the Celts

The hazel was the tree of poetry, fire, fertility and wisdom; the famous Celtic salmon of inspiration gained his wisdom from eating the nuts of the hazel as they fell into the pool below.

Common Vervain. It has delicate, sparse branches and pale mauve flowers, July–September

The Apple tree, which was sacred to the Mother Goddess, grew around the Arthurian isle of Avalon, and 'Purple crested' apple trees were to be found in the earthly paradise of Emhain, where there were also 'Horses of golden yellow there on the meadow, other horses of purple colour; other noble horses beyond them, of the colour of the all-blue sky'.
From 'The Islands of the Earthly Paradise', Irish, 7th–8th century, author unknown.

Celtic Beauty

'The colour of her hair seemed to them like the flower of the water-flag in summer, or like red gold that has been polished ... Her upper arms were as white as the snow of a single night ... her clear and lovely cheeks were as red as the foxglove of the moor ...'
From 'Edaín the Fairy', 9th century Irish, Anon.

'... Her head was yellower than the flowers of the broom; her flesh was whiter than the foam of the waves; her palms and fingers were whiter than the flowers of the melilot among the small pebbles of a gushing spring ... redder than the foxglove were her cheeks ...'
From 'Olwen', 10th century Welsh, Anon.

The Celtic goddess Blodeuwedd, which means 'flower-face', was created in the following way:
'... they took the flowers of the oak-trees and the flowers of the broom and the flowers of the meadowsweet, and out of these they created the fairest and most perfect girl that man had ever seen ...'
Welsh, author unknown, 11th century (?)

The Lay of the Nine Herbs

The Anglo-Saxon 'Lay of the Nine Herbs' is an eleventh- or twelfth-century poem about the ancient herbs of power. It says: 'Now these nine worts avail Gainst nine exiles from glory, Gainst nine venoms, and nine flying vile things ...' Of the nine herbs, or 'worts', described only six have been identified. They are: Mugwort, or *Artemesia vulgaris*, which was sacred to Artemis, goddess of the Moon, and grows along the wayside offering protection to travellers; a leaf picked before sunrise and carried on a journey will prevent any weariness. It is the 'Eldest of Worts', and 'Of might against the vile She who fares through the land,' that is, against evil spirits.

Plantain, or 'waybroad' is the next herb mentioned in the poem. It is addressed thus:

'Over thee carts creaked,
Over thee queens rode,
Over thee brides bridalled,
Over thee bulls breathed,
All these thou withstoodst ... '

The plantain is still used to cure bruises; as it springs up unharmed when crushed it has a reputation for helping anyone crushed or bruised to do the same.

The next herb that has been identified is 'Maythe', which is either chamomile or its cousin the Stinking Mayweed. Fennel, Sweet Cicely and apples complete the list of recognisable plants; the other three remain a mystery.

The nine herbs are to be gathered while the proper charm is recited over each in turn; it must then be sung into the mouth and ears of the wounded man, and into his wound, while the herbs are made up into a salve and applied to the wound.

Charms, Fertility and Divinations of True Love

May Day

May Day, which really falls on May 13th, when the pink and white Hawthorn is in full bloom along the hedgerows, is the first day of summer. Only in the eighteenth century, with the change in the

May Queen

calendar, did it fall on the 1st, as we know it now, at which time the Hawthorn is rarely in blossom. It was the time when the fertility of the earth was awakening after the long winter, and it needed protection from the witches and fairies who were much in evidence at that time of year. Their evil influence

was averted by the sacred plants of the May, which were Hawthorn, Marsh Marigolds, and in the north, the Rowan tree.

Garlands of Hawthorn, or May, were hung up outside the doors of houses to prevent any evil from entering, but it was never brought indoors, and it is still considered unlucky to do so. The Puritans abhorred these May Day customs; and to some the slightly stale, sickening smell of May blossom is supposed to be reminiscent of sex. It is one of the flowers with which the May Pole was decked before it was carried in from the woods, and the weaving dance around the May Pole guaranteed the fertility of nature for the coming year.

To Conceive a Child

At Padstow, a small fishing port on the north coast of Cornwall, the May Day festivities are still celebrated in the old style; the May Pole is decked with bunches of bluebells and cowslips, the young men of the town wear white clothes with red satin sashes and red and white bandanas – the colours of death and rebirth – and a procession meanders slowly through the town headed by the Padstow hobby horse. If you wish to conceive a child that year, legend has it that you must get caught beneath his skirts as he passes.

Midsummer's Eve

Midsummer's Eve, or St John's Eve as it used to be called, falls on June 23. It is the witching hour for all love matters, and there are many plants associated with it. These should be gathered at dawn with

Dancing round the May Pole

the dew still on them, and smoked in the Midsummer bonfires that night. They will then preserve their magical powers throughout the year.

To marry within the Year, and dream that Night of your Future Husband

Go out at dawn, fasting, on St John's Eve, and gather a plant of St John's Wort* with the dew still on it, and you will marry before Midsummer's Eve comes round again. That evening place it under your pillow, preferably smoked in the Midsummer bonfire, and your future husband will appear to you in a dream.

A Cure for Barrenness

To conceive a child within the year you must walk naked in your garden at dawn, and pick St John's Wort.

To conjure up a Midnight Vision of your True Love

As the clock is about to strike midnight on Midsummer's Eve go out into the garden and pluck twelve sage leaves: one as each note strikes, being careful not to damage any of them. Your future husband will then appear, walking up silently behind you. This is only recommended for those with strong nerves. If you then find yourself locked out of the house, you must find a sprig of Moonwort, which may not be easy as its existence seems uncertain, and press it to the lock, when the door will magically spring open.

* St John's Wort, or *Hypericum perforatum*, is a cousin of the garden flower called Rose of Sharon. It has golden flowers that have long, fluffy stamens like a crown, and it is common on lime soil.

To regain your Lover's Affections

Pick three rose buds on Midsummer's Eve, and bury one in a newly made grave, another under a Yew tree, and the third under your pillow. Your lover's sleep will be wracked with dreams about you, and he will get no rest until he returns.

To know if Two People will love Each Other

Take two sprigs of Orpine, and lay them side by side in a warm place. If after a period of time they have inclined towards one another the two people that they have been chosen to represent will love one another; if they bend away from each other they will not. This must be done on St John's Eve. Orpine was often woven into garlands with corn marigolds, another Midsummer flower.

'A Midsummer Night's Dream'

The pansy, or Heart's Ease, which used to grow wild in the fields in Culpeper's time, is supposed to be the 'love-in-idleness' of 'A Midsummer Night's Dream'. Its juice, squeezed by Puck into the eyes of the sleeping Titania, made her fall in love with the first person she saw when she awoke. It is also sacred to St Valentine.

Legend has it that the pansy was once white; Cupid aimed his bow at the chaste goddess Diana, but the arrow glanced off her and wounded a pansy at her feet.

Other plants of St John's Eve are Fennel; Bracken, which reveals 'a certaine forme of a spred Eagle' if 'cut aslope', according to Gerard; Ivy, a plant of Dionysius; ox-eye daisies, Mugwort, and Male Fern and Vervain which are both thought to possess aphrodisiac qualities, and Yarrow.

Titania and Bottom

Other Charms

A Charm using Yarrow

> Yarrow, sweet Yarrow, the first that I have found
> In the name of Jesus Christ, I pluck you from the ground.
> As Jesus loved sweet Mary, and took her for his dear,
> So in a dream this night, I hope my true love will appear.

This rhyme must be recited over the Yarrow as it is picked, and it must then be placed under the pillow to procure a dream of your True Love.

It was also used to protect a new born baby's cradle from evil.

To make your True Love appear in a Dream

Go to a graveyard you have never visited before, pick a sprig of Yew, and sleep with it under your pillow; you will dream of your true love.

To make your True Love appear

Sit on a chair with a mirror behind you and a mirror in front of you, and eat an apple. Your true love will appear walking up the endless corridor in the mirrors.

A Mirror and the Moon

To know how many years you have to go before you marry, stand on a stone you have never stood on before with your back to the full moon, holding a mirror in your hand; you will see the moon's reflection in the mirror with a series of smaller moons. Each miniature moon represents a year.

Love Potions

'For making the True Love Powder'

'Take elecampane, the seeds or flowers, vervain, and the berries of mistletoe. Beat them, after being well dried in an oven, into a powder, and give it to the party you design upon in a glasse of wine and it will work wonderful effect to your advantage'. From the pseudo-Aristotle's *Golden Cabinet of Secrets*. *Warning:* mistletoe berries are poisonous, so leave them out.

To ensure a Happy Marriage

Dip sprigs of rosemary into the newly married couple's wine for certain love and happiness.

Mugwort is slightly aromatic. It grows in waste places and by the wayside, reaching a height of 3 feet. It has a reddish stalk and leaves which are green above and white beneath. It has small brown flowers from July to September

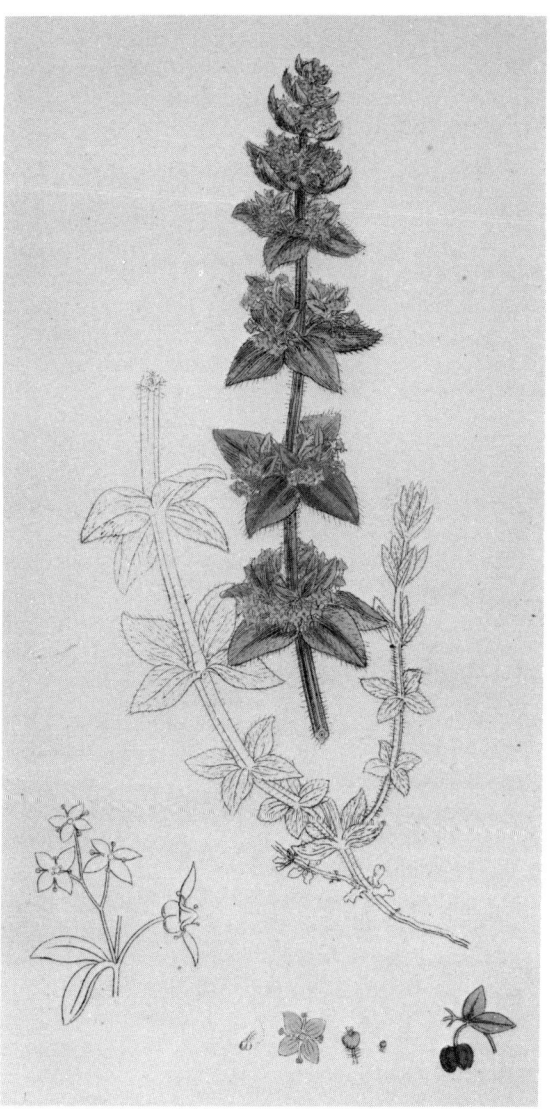

Myrtle Water

The myrtle is sacred to Venus, and was supposed to have been used by her to enhance her beauty. Here is a recipe:

'A curious Water of Mirtle Flowers'

'The flowers and leaves of mirtle, two handfuls, infuse them in two quarts of spring water, and a quart of white wine, twenty four hours, and then distil them in a cold still and this will be of a strong scent and tincture, and by adding more or less of the mirtle you may make it stronger or weaker as you please. This beautifies, and mixed with cordial syrups is a good cordial and inclines those that drink it to be very amorous.'

A mixture of coriander, violet and valerian will produce love if they are gathered in the last quarter of the moon, according to the pseudo-Albertus Magnus. *Warning:* go very easy on the valerian, which is a narcotic.

Mandrake and Bryony

Mandrake, probably owing to the shape of its roots, which resemble the lower half of a man's body, was long considered to be amongst other things, a cure for sterility and barrenness. It must be picked in the following way: once the mandrake has been found, a hungry dog must be tethered to the plant and some food placed just out of his reach. Eventually the dog will wrench up the mandrake by the roots, which will give an unearthly shriek and the dog will go mad. The point of this strange and ruthless behaviour is to obtain a mandrake root without going mad oneself.

Bryony is described by Jeffries in *Wild Life in a Southern County*: 'The white bryony, whose leaf is not unlike that of the grape, has a magical reputation, and the cottage folk believe its root to be a powerful ingredient in love potions, and also poisonous. They identify it with the mandrake. If growing in or close to a churchyard, its virtues are increased, for, though becoming fainter as they

Sea Holly

lengthen, the shadows of the old superstitions linger still.' It was known as 'mandrake' or 'womandrake' depending on the shape of the root, and was used as an aphrodisiac and to ensure fertility, men eating womandrake, and vice versa. The dose was a small amount of the root, powdered. *Warning: it is poisonous.*

Kissing Comfits

The Elizabethans were very fond of the candied roots of Sea Holly, or Eryngo, which they believed had aphrodisiac qualities, hence their name.

Eryingo roots can be bought at Culpeper's, but they are broken into small pieces, and so would be difficult to candy; a decoction of the roots can be made and drunk as a tea instead.

Lettuce

Wild and garden lettuce have both been considered aphrodisiac and narcotic; they are also said to promote child bearing. In France a herbal infusion is sometimes given as a mild sedative.

Oranges and Orange Blossom

Both the fruit and flowers of the orange tree were considered to have the power to secure love, a belief which made a wreath of orange blossom the most popular wreath for brides. In Norfolk the gift of an orange was supposed to win the love of the person who received it.

Other Plants used in Love Potions

Dill; cyclamen, which not only caused passionate love, but was also supposed to help girls recover from the shock of being jilted; pansies, carrots, henbane, cinnamon, ginger, Belladonna, and cubebs. Henbane and Belladonna are both poisonous.

'Against the Raging Disease of Love'

'It is a doubt whether the seat of this ill be in the brain or the liver, but in either case the patient will do wisely to administer to himself a cooling clyster of hempseed and bruised cucumber and follow this after a brief interval with thin potations of waterlilies and purslane and let him drive at it last of all with a strong pinch of snuff of the herb Hanea.' Aetius.

Although Avicenna and Galen advised applying a poultice of Hemlock to cure love, it is extremely poisonous, so don't try it. Poppies have also been considered helpful, but they too are poisonous.

To cease Weeping

'Make a little plaster of small powder of henbane seed and of whites of eggs, of vinegar and of woman's milk and of incense and lay it to the head and to the stomach.' From a Fifteenth-Century Leechbook.

Henbane is also poisonous.

If all else fails, you could try

Homer's Nepenthe

which, according to Pliny and Dioscorides, was made of borage steeped in wine, and brought complete forgetfulness.

Appendix: Metric Conversion Tables

To convert ounces to grammes multiply by 28·35
To convert grammes to ounces multiply by 0·035
To convert quarts to litres multiply by 1·14
To convert fluid ounces to millilitres multiply by 0·0285
To convert litres to quarts multiply by 0·88

Ounces and Pounds to Grammes

Ounces	Pounds	Grammes	(Actual)
1		30	(28·35)
3		85	(85·05)
4	¼	115	(113·4)
5		140	(141·8)
6		170	(170·1)
8	½	225	(226·8)
9		250	(255·2)
10		285	(283·5)
12	¾	340	(340·2)
16	1	450	(453·6)
20	1¼	560	(566·99)
24	1½	675	(680·4)
28	1¾	800	(794)
32	2	900	(908)
40	2½	1125	(1134)
48	3	1350	(1360)
56	3½	1500	(1588)
64	4	1800	(1814)

Fluid Ounces and Pints to Litres

Fluid ounces	Pints	Decilitres	Litres	Millilitres
1		¼		28·5
2		½		57
3		¾		86
4	⅕	1		114
5	¼	1½		143
6		1¾		171
8			¼	228
10	½	3		285
12		3½		342
14		4		399
15	¾	4¼		428
16			½	456
20	1	5¾		570
24	1⅕	6¾		684
25	1¼		¾	713
30	1½	8½		855
35	1¾		1	998
40	2		1·1	1140
50	2½		1½	1425
60	3		1¾	1710
80	4		2¼	2280

1 ounce	= 1 tablespoon	lb	= pound	qt	= quart
1 pint	= 20 fluid ounces	oz	= ounce	l	= litre
1 quart	= 2 pints	g	= gramme	dl	= decilitre
1 litre	= 1000 ml, 10 dl.	tbs	= tablespoon	ml	= millilitre
1 decilitre	= $\frac{1}{10}$ litre	pt	= pint	1000 g	= 1 kilogramme

Picture Credits and Acknowledgments

Pictures on pp. 16, 24, 29, 35, 36, 42, 45, 51, 56, 64, 66, 68, 75, 83, 84, 99, 103 and 120 are reproduced from *A Modern Herbal* by Mrs M. Grieve, Jonathan Cape, 1931; the picture on p. 26 is from *The Wild Garland* by S. Waring, Harvey and Darton, 1827. For permission to reproduce other pictures the author and publishers are grateful to: B.B.C. Hulton Picture Library, pp. 9, 11, 21, 39, 48, 52, 59, 73, 76, 85, 86, 87, 95, 105, 109, 112, 116; Mary Evans Picture Library, frontispiece, pp. 7, 30, 32, 33, 41, 43, 44, 53, 57, 61, 62, 69, 70, 78, 94, 96, 100, 107, 115; the Mansell Collection, pp. 14, 23, 25, 31, 47, 49, 54, 82, 92, 93, 102, 106, 111, 113, 114, 118, 119, and the borders on pp. 11, 21, 39, 59, 73, 79, 97, 109; a private collection and The Bucentaur Gallery, p. 97.

A Select Bibliography

CULPEPER, NICHOLAS, *Culpeper's Complete Herbal*, W. Foulsham.

GRIEVE, MRS M., *A Modern Herbal*, Jonathan Cape 1931, reprinted 1974

GRIGSON, GEOFFREY, *The Englishman's Flora*, Paladin, 1975 (first published by Phoenix House, 1958)

— *A Herbal of All Sorts*, Phoenix House, 1959

KEBLE MARTIN, W., *The Concise British Flora in Colour*, Ebury Press and Michael Joseph, 1976

LEYEL, HILDA, *The Magic of Herbs*, Jonathan Cape, 1926

PIESSE, G. W. S., *Piesse's Art of Perfumery*, Piesse and Lubin, 1891

RENDALL, VERNON, *Wild Flowers in Literature*, Scholartis Press, 1934

ROSE, JEANNE, *The Herbal Body Book*, Grosset and Dunlap, 1976

SANDERSON, LIZ, *Herbal Cosmetics*, Fontana 1979 (first published by Latimer New Dimensions, 1977)

STAFFE, BARONESS, *The Lady's Dressing Room*, 1892

TISSERAND, ROBERT, *Aromatherapy*, Mayflower Books, 1979

THOMPSON, C. J. S., *The Mystery and Lure of Perfume*, Bodley Head, 1927

Index

(Page numbers in bold refer to illustrations.)

A Rebours (Huysmans): *quoted*, 95
Aches and Pains, bath for, 47
Achilles, **32**, 32
Adonis, 26
Aegyptium, 83
Aetius: *quoted*, 121
aftershaves, 20
agar, agar, 34, 35, 49, 51
alchemy, 15
Alexis the Piedmontese, 15, 33, 103
alkanet, 13, 37, 69, 70, 75, 87
allspice berries, 33, 100
almond, 35, 35; and Honey Mask, 35; oil, 13, 29, 30, 31, 32, 36, 37, 44, 48, 50, 64, 77, 86; Paste, 54–5
alum, 72
ambergris, 88, 90, 92, **93**, 94
Anatomy of Melancholy (Burton): *quoted*, 108
Andropogon Schoenanthus, 81
Angelic Water, 36
Anglo-Saxons, 26, 32, 46, 114
Anne of Austria, 38, **54**, 54–5, 71
antimony, 13
aphrodisiacs, 107, 113, 117, 120
Apollo, 31, 31
apple(s), 13, 87, 115, 119; blossom oil, 44; juice, 34; trees, 113, 114
apricot kernel oil, 44, 49
aromatherapy, 46, 48, 49
Art of Perfumery (Piesse): *quoted*, 91
Artificial Embellishments (Jameson): *quoted*, 77
ash tree, 113
astringents, 20, 24, 26, 28, 29, 30, 32–4
astrology, 13
Avicenna, 88, 121
avocado oil, 44, 49, 50

Babylon, 13; Hanging Gardens of, 81, 82, 85; perfume of, 84–5
Bain Marie, 18
balsam, *see* benzoin
balsam poplar, 101
barberry, 66
basil, 43
bath(s), 41–3; bag, 46, 47, 48; herbs and flowers in, 46–8; oils, 43–5
bay, 45, 47, 48, 63, 66, 96, 101, 108; Cream, 31; salt, 99, 100–1
bdellium, 81
beauty: and alchemy, 15; and astrology, 13–15; historic ideas about, 13, 37, 41–2, 81–8, 89, 91–6, 114
beeswax, 18, 29, 30, 32, 36, 37, 38, 50, 52, 76, 77
Beeton, Mrs, 33
beetroot juice, 37
belladonna, 121
benjamin, *see* benzoin
benzoin (balsam, benjamin), 35–7, **36**, 88, 92, 96, 100, 101, 104
bergamot, 44, 45, 49, 50, 57, 86, 90, 94, 95, 100, 103, 106
Best Way Book, The: *quoted*, 76, 77
Biblical Bath Oil, 45
blackberry leaves, 28
bladderwrack, 51
blinds, scent for, 106–7
bluebells, 116
borage, 99, 101, 121
borax, 50, 52, 56, 57
bracken, 117
broom, 68, **99**, 99
bryony, 120–1
burdock root, 65

calamus (sweet rush), 42, 54, 81, 84, 84, 87, 92, 100, 102, 104, 108
camphire, *see* henna
Campion, Thomas: *quoted*, 21
candles, scent for, 108
Capelli Fila d'Oro, 67–8
caraway, 57
Carnation, 46; Mixture, A Spicy, 101
carrots, 121
cassia, 57, 81, 84, 88
castus, 88
cedar: oil of, 81; wood, 45, 49, 57, 106
celandine, 23
Celestial Water, 36
Celts, 112–14

chamomile, **16**, 28, 29, 38, 49, 52, 54, 63, 64, 65, 102, 107, 115; Cream, 29; Dye, 69, 70–1; Marigold and Quassia Rinse, 71
Chaplet of Herbs, A: *quoted*, 46, 71, 77
Charles V, King of France, **49**, bath of, 48
Charles VI, King of France, 107
charms, 115–19; for conception, 116, 117, 120, 121
Chaucer, Geoffrey: *quoted*, 25
chilblains, to prevent, 78
China Ink, 95
Chinese aids to beauty, 37, 65
cicely, sweet, 115
cinnamon, 13, 37, 38, 42, 45, 57, 78, 81, 84, 88, 100, 101, 104, 121; white, 83
cistus, 45, 101
citronella, 44, 45, 50, 51; Scented Candle, 108
civet, 90, **93**, 93, 94, 106
clary sage, 44, 90, 95, 100
Cleopatra, Queen of Egypt, 13, 42, 81
clothes, scent for, 104–6
clove, 57, 69, 72, 95, 96, 100, 101, 104
clover, 46
cochineal, 38
cocoa butter, 18, 30, 31, 37, 41, 50, 52
coconut oil, 29, 44, 50
coffee grounds, 69
Cold Cream, Galen's, 30
Columbus, Christopher, **44**, 44
comfrey, 28, 31, 46, 50, 64; and sunburn, 51
complexion: bad, remedies for, 25, 27; cleansing of, 28–9; waters for, 23–7; *see also* skin
coriander, 81, 92, 104
cornflowers, 99, 101; Water of, 27
cosmetics: making, 17–18; *see also* individual items
costmary, 28
Cottage Garden Bath, 47–8
coumarin, 102, 108
cowslip flowers, 29, 116
creams, 29–32; making, 17, 18
crocuses, 13, 87; saffron, **68**, 83, 86, 88, 89
cucumber, 26, 121
Culpeper, Nicholas, 24, 26, 34, 52, 67, 117
cushions, scent for, 107
cyclamen, 121

125

cyperus, 81
cypress: oil of, 81; wood, 49, 104
cyprinum, 81, 84

daisy(ies), 46; ox-eye, 117; Water, 25
Damask Powder, 104
Danewort, 65
Daphne, 31
decoction, 19
Delights for Ladies (Sir Hugh Platt): quoted, 27
deodorants, herbal, 48
dill, 66, 121
Dioscorides, 81
distillation, 15, 17, 19, 90–1; prolonging life of distilled waters, 19–20
distilled water, 69
Doctrine of Signatures, The, 14, 25
Druids, 111, 112, 112–13
dyes (hair), 65, 67–72; blonde, 70–2; brown, 72; red, 67; strawberry blonde, 70

East, scents of The, 88
Eau de Ange, 85
Eau de Chypre, 13, 91–2
Eau de Cologne, 81, 94; Pot Pourri, 103
Eau de Millefleurs, 92
Eau de Toilette (floral waters), 15, 89–91, 96
Eden, Garden of, 84–5
Edward VI, Rose, scent of, 108
egg, 34, 62, 65, 68, 121
Egypt, Ancient: dye, 75; perfumes of, 13, 31, 41, 78, 81–3, 86
elder: berry, 38, 72; dwarf, 65; leaves, 27; tree, 24–5, 68
elderflower: Ointment, 32, 77; Water, 24–5, 51
elecampane, 46, 119
Elizabeth I: perfumes of, 93, 104; red hair of, 67
Elizabeth, Queen of Hungary, 13, 92, 92, 93
Emerson, Ralph Waldo: quoted, 11
enfleurage, 15, 90, 91
Ethyl alcohol (ethanol), 15, 20, 36, 42, 55, 85, 88, 89, 91, 92, 93, 94, 95, 96
Exodus: quoted, 84
Eyebright Lotion, 27
eyes: bloodshot, 24; to brighten, 27; weak, 27

Farina, John Maria, 94
feet, 77–8; toenails, 78
fennel, 23, 115, 117
fern, male, 117
fixatives, for pot pourri, 100–1
floors, scent for, 108
floral waters, *see* Eau de Toilette
flowers: drying, 15, 99; *see also individual names*
Flowery Vinegar Astringent, 33
Frangipani, 44; tree, 45, 93
frankincense, 13, **45**, 45, 49, 81, 86
freckles, remedies for, 24, 27
fuller's earth, 34, 35

galbanum, 45
Galen (herbalist), **30**, 30, 81, 87, 121
galingale, 81, 104
gardenia, 43, 44
geranium: leaves, 33, 45, 101; oil, 38, 51, 96; rose, 28, 29, 47, 55, 96
Gerard (herbalist), 52, 108, 117
gillyflower, scent, 87
giner, 121
ginseng, 50
glycerin, 20, 33, 34, 49, 51, 76
Golden Cabinet of Secrets: quoted, 119
Greece, Ancient: hair dyes of, 72; perfumes of, 13, 41, 85–7; rouge of, 37
Green Pot Pourri, 101
Grigson, Geoffrey, 53

Hafiz, *The Rubaiyat:* quoted, 88
hair, 59–72; bad condition of, 64–5; to curl, 65; dry, 64, 65; falling, 66; greasy, 63, 65; growth of, 63, 65, 66; weak, 62
hands, 73–7; fingernails, 75–6; red, 76; soft, 77
hawthorn, 113, 115–16
hazel, 113
headaches, remedy for, 26
Helen of Troy, 13, 46
hemlock, 121
Hemsia (Almond Paste), 54–5
henbane, 121
henna (camphire), 68–9, 75, 81, 85; Neutral, 65
Henry, King of France, Violette Powder for linen of, 104
herbs: distilling, 17; and Druids, 112–13; drying, 15; foot bath, 78; infusing, 17, 18–19, 28–9; magical, 13, 111; soft

soap, of, 56–7; *see also individual names*
hibiscus, 38, 45, 69
Hildegarde, Saint, 92
hollyhock(s), 46, 99; Cream, 30
Homer: Nepenthe, 121; *The Odyssey:* quoted, 75
honey, 34, 43, 55, 66, 83; and Almond Mask, 35; and Lemon Soap, 56
honeysuckle, 43
hops, 107
horehound, white, 75, 75
Horse Chestnut Paste, 77
houseleek, 43, 46
Hovenia, 95, 96
'Huiles Antiques', 30, 43, 45, 86
Hungary Water, 13, 92, 94
hyacinths, 87, 93
hyssop, 45, 46, 47

illnesses: germ killer for, 103–4; old remedies for, 112–13; plague, 103
India, 31, 85, 88
Indian: Bath Oil, 45; jatamansi (nard), 83; Shawls, 104–5; Vetivert blinds, 106–7
infusions, 18–19, 28–9
insect repellents, 50; Anti-Mosquito Splash, 51; candle, 108; oil, 50; sachets, 104, 105, 106
Ipswich Ball, 58
irises, 13, 86, 87, 108
Irish moss, 34, 35, 51
Irish myths: quoted, 114
Isabella, Queen of Spain, 105; Sachet Powder of, 104
Islands of the Earthly Paradise: quoted, 114
Israel, Ancient, perfumes of, 84
ivy, 117; essence of ground, 87

jasmine, 45, 46, 90, 94, 101, 103, 107; oil, 15, 36, 37, 92; and Orange Blossom Powder, 53; pommade, 36
June Water, 27
juniper, 81–2, 103, 108; berries, 47, 104

kaolin, 53, 54, 71
kohl, 13
Koran, 89
Kyphi, 81–3

labdanum, 104

Lady's Dressing Room (Staffe), 71; quoted, 38, 96, 105
lady's mantle, 28, 52–3
Lady's Toilette: quoted, 36, 55, 61, 75, 77
lanolin, 18, 29, 30, 34, 35, 55, 77
lard, 32, 37, 41, 91
lavender, 28, 30, 38, 43, 44, 45, 46, 47, 49, 57, 63, 87, 90, 91, 94, 95, 99, 103, 104, 106, 107, 108; Cream, 29–30; and Orris Powder, 53; spike, **29**; Water, 25–6, 33, 36, 81, 92, 94
Lay of the Nine Herbs: quoted, 114–15
Leechbook: quoted, 121
lemon, **66**, 90; juice, 29, 34, 66, 69, 76; leaves, 45, 102, 103; oil ot, 56, 93, 94, 96; peel, 54, 100, 101, 103, 104
lemon balm, 33, 46, 48, 56, 93, 101
lemon grass, 44, 81
lemon verbena, 45, 56, 101, 107, 113
lettuce, 121; Juice, 26
lilies, 43, 44, 45, 85, 86
lime blossom, 28, 46, 54, 63, 107
linseed, 43
lipstick, 37–8
liquorice: root, 28; sticks, 35
lotions, 17, 18, 30–1, 50, 51
lovage, 46, 47, 48
love: charms, 111, 117–19; potions, 26, 111, 113, 119–21
lupins, 46

mace, 100, 101
maceration, 87
magic and plants, 109–21
maidenhair fern, 65
make-up, 37–8
mallow, 30; Hand Cream, 77; Marsh, **42**, 43
mandrake, 120
Marie Antoinette, 71, 93–4; bath of, 48
marigold, 28, 29, 46, 47, 54, 99, 101; Chamomile, and Quassia Rinse, 71; corn, 117; Cream, 29–30; Hair Rinse, 69–70; Marsh, 116
marjoram, 13, 48, 86, 87, 104
Marvell, Andrew: quoted, 35
Mary Queen of Scots, 42
masks, face, 34–5
massage oils, 48–9
mastic, 83, 88
May: Day, 115, **116**, 115–16; Dew, 23, 23, 111

meadowsweet, 46, 47, 105, 108
Medebathrim, 88
Mediterranean Bath Oil, 45
melilot, 102, 105
mendes, 88
Mendesium, 83
Mercury, 25–6
Metopium, 83
Middle Ages, The: face powder of, 37; perfumes of, 91–3; and red hair, 67
A Midsummer Night's Dream, 9, 117, 118
Midsummer's Eve: charms, 116–17
mignonette, 47, 90, 105
Milk Bath, 42, 43
mimosa, 45
mint, 28, 29, 34, 46, 47, 86, 101; water, 108; wild, 13, 87
mistletoe, 111, 112–13, 119
Mohammed, 68, 81, 85, 89
Moon, 26, 83, 111, 114, 119
Moonwort, 117
Mousseline des Indes, 107
Montpellier, herbes de, 107
mugwort, 114–15, 117, **119**
musk, 37, 88, 89, 90, 92, 93, 94, 104, 106
myrrh, 13, 42, 45, 83, 84, 88; Cream, 31; oil of, 81, 100
myrtle, 85, 87; Water, 120

Nani, Contessa, 67
Napoleon Bonaparte, 57, 94; soap of, 57
narcissus, 42, 87; essence of, 87–8
narcotics, 26, 113, 120, 121
Nardinum, 88
Nebuchadnezzar, King of Babylon, 85
Neck Cream, 50
Nefertiti, Queen of Egypt, 81
neroli, see orange blossom
nettle, 14, 46, 63, 65, 66, 77
New-Mown Hay, 102, 108; pot pourri, 102; Powder, 54
Ninon de l'Enclos's Bath, 43
nutmeg, 100, 101

oak, 112; leaves, 48
oatmeal, dry, 77
ochre, red, 13
oils; bath, 43–6; essential, 15, 16, 18, 44, 90; Holy Anointing, 84; insect repellent, 50; massage, 48–9; scented Grecian, 86; sun, 50; synthetic, 15

olive oil, 30, 50, 65, 84; soap, 62, 63, 64, 69
Onegalium, 88
orange, 128; blossom (neroli), 33, 43, 44, 45, 50, 51, 64, 65, 91, 93, 94, 95, 96, 102, 103, 121; and Jasmine Powder, 53; Groves (pot pourri), 102–3; peel, 37, 94, 100
origanum, 13
orpine, 117
orris, 37, 38, 92, 93, 96, 100, 101, 104, 107; and Lavender, 53
Ovid: metamorphoses, 35

Padstow hobby horse, 116
Paestum, Temples of, 13, 87, 87
pansies, 78, 99, 101, 117, 121
parsley seeds, 66
patchouli, 45, 95; leaves, 104–5
peach kernel oil, 48–9, 86
pennyroyal, 77; Vinegar, 34
peppermint, 34, 83; oil, 49, 93; Shampoo for Greasy Hair, 63–4
perfumes, see scent
Periwinkle Water, 26, 32
petitgrain, 45, 57, 63, 94, 103
Piesse, Septimus, 31, 50, 105, 107; Art of Perfumery: quoted, 91, 108
pillows, scent for, 107
pimpernel, scarlet, **24**; Water, 24, 32
pine-apple kernels, 43
pinks, 99, 101; Powder, 53–4; Water of, 96
plantain, 115; greater, **25**; Water, 25, 32
Plutarch: quoted, 81
poisonous plants, 14, 119, 120, 121
Poitiers, Diane de, **48**; bath of, 48
pomanders, 93
Pomegranate Juice, 26–7
Pompadour, Madame de, 93
poppy, 121; red, **26**; Turkish, Water, 27
pot pourris, 97–104
powder: Medieval Face, 37; Rice 38; Talcum, 53–4
pregnancy: breasts, 52; charms for conception, 116, 117, 120, 121; stretch marks, 51–2
preservatives: chemical, 20; vitamin E, 18; wheatgerm oil, 18
Princess of Wales (skin lotion), 32
privet, 67, 72
Proserpine, 27

127

pumice stone, 78
Puritans, 116

quassia, 63, **64**, 64, 70; Chamomile, Marigold and, Rinse, 71
Queen's Closet Opened, The (1655): quoted, 58, 108
quince, 34, 35, 42, 49, 51, 72, 87

radish, 67
Ram's Little Dodoen (1606): *quoted*, 23, 57, 107
raspberry juice, 43
Receipt Book of John Nott, The (1723): quoted, 58
Red Indians, 25
refrigeration, 20, 51
Renaissance, herbalists of, 13–14
Rhodium (Rose Unguent), 41–2
rhubarb, 67
rice powder, 38
rinses (hair), 65; colour, 67, 69–70, 71
Rome, Ancient: baths of, 25, **41**, 41, **43**; Dog Days in, 113; hair dyes of, 71–2; perfumes of, 83, 87–8; vervain (Verbena) used in, 113
Rondeletia, 95
rooms, scent for, 108
rose(s), 43, 45, 46, 47, 85, 86, 87, 90, 93, 94; attar of, 13, 88, 89, 107; buds, 117; extract, 85; oil, 15, 30, 38, 41, 49, 69, 87, 92, 93, 95, 96; of Paestum and Phaselis, 13, 87; petals, 28, 41, 53, 101, 103, 105; Pot Pourri, 101–2; preserving, 89; Scent for Rooms, 108; Tea, 96; Unguent (Rhodium), 41–2; Water, 33, 34, 35, 36, 37, 41, 55, 88, 93, 104; White, Sachet, 105; wine of, 41; wood, 106
rosemary, 33, 43, 49, **56**, 56, 57, 63, 64, 65, 66, 77, 93, 94, 101, 103, 107, 119
rouge, 36–7
Rousseau, *quoted*, 79
Rowan, 116
rue, 77
rush, sweet, *see* calamus

sachets, 104–6
saffron, 42, 68, 83, 86, 88, 89
sage, 56, 63, 72, 93, 117
St John's Eve, *see* Midsummer's Eve

St John's Wort, 46, 117
Salernum, The School of, 66
salt, 43; bay, 99, 100–1; sea, 48
sandalwood, 45, 49, 50, 96, 100, 104, 106, 107; Lotion, 30–1
Saturn, 28
scent, 15, 41–2, 79–96; dry, 104–8; history of, 81–8, 89, 91–6
Schnouda ('Arabian Nights' rouge), 13, 36–7
sea holly (eryngo), **120**, 121
seaweed bath, 51
sesame oil, 44
shampoos, 18, 61–4, 69
shells, scented, 106
skin, 29, 30, 34; damaged, 24, 25, 28, 30, 31, 32, 36; disinfectant for, 26, 28, 36; dry, 20, 28, 32–3, 34; oily, 20, 26, 28, 33–4, 35; rough, 48, 50; sallow, 28–9; sensitive, 20, 28, 32–3
sleep, aids to, 26, 107
soaps, 18, 55–8, 62
soapwort root, 62
soda, carbonate of, 43
Song of Solomon, 31, 81: *quoted*, 84
southernwood, 63, 66
spikenard, 42, 83, 86
spots, remedies for, 24, 26, 28
Staffe, Baroness: *Lady's Dressing Room*, 71, 77: quoted, 38, 96, 105
stockists, 16–17, 49, 89, 90, 121
Strawberry: juice, 43, 78; Wild, Water, 27
suet, 32
Summer: Bath, 47; High Bath, 46–7
sunburn, 26, 51; oil, 50
sunflower seed oil, 44
Susinum, 42, 88
sweet pea, 90
sweet vernal grass, 102, 108
Sweet William, 101

talcum powder, 53–4
Tallier's Bath, Mme, 43
tangerine peel, 100
tea, Indian, 72
theobroma, oil of, *see* cocoa butter
thyme, 43, 48, 56, 77, 86, 101, 104, 107; wild, 45, 48, 87
tomato juice, 34
tonquin beans, 54, 92, 100, 102

Tropical Bath Oil, 44–5
Trotula of Salerno, 68
tuberose, 45, 91; oil, 15, 104
Tudors: perfumes of, 93, 108; and sea holly, 121
Turkey Red oil, 44

unguents, 41–2
utensils, 17, 38, 53, 56, 57, 90

valerian, 120
vanilla, 38, 44, 55, 100, 102; oil, 50, 92, 95
Vaseline, 37, 38, 77, 78
Venice, 67; Water, 36
Venus, 2, 24, 25, 67, 71, 120
verbena, 93, 104
vervain, 46, **113**, 113, 117, 119
Vetivert, 106–7
Victorian: perfumes, 95–6, 105, 106; rouge, 37
Vine: leaves, 47, 86; Tears of the, 27; tendrils, 66
vinegar, white wine, 33, 34
violet, 44, 86, 87, 90, 93, 105, 120; Sorcerer's, Water of, 26
Virgil, 53
Virgin Milk, 36
vitamin E, 18, 29, 30, 31, 32, 44, 49, 50, 52, 77, 86

wallflower, 87, 94, 99, 101, 104
walnut, 72; oil, 64
Wars of the Roses (bath), 47
Waters, for complexion, 23–7
Welsh myth: *quoted*, 114
wheatgerm oil, *see* vitamin E
Wild Life in a Southern Country (Jeffries): *quoted*, 120–1
Wilde, Oscar: *quoted*, 96
wine, 67, 77, 83, 119, 120, 121
witch-hazel, 33, 65; Cream, 31; and sunburn, 51
woodruff, sweet, 50, 102, 105
writing paper, scent for, 106

yarrow, **33**, 63, 117, 118; Cream, 32; Water, 32
yew, 117, 118
ylang ylang, 44, 50